A Mother's Prayer

The Hidden Power That Shapes Generations

Gerard Assey

A Mother's Prayer:
The Hidden Power That Shapes Generations

By

Gerard Assey

Published by:
Gerard Assey
19/18, Palli Arasan Street
Anna Nagar East
Chennai - 600 102

ISBN: 978-81-69340-40-3

Table of Contents

DEDICATION

This book is lovingly dedicated to my wife, June Assey — a true Proverbs 31 woman, a praying mother, a faithful builder of our home, and now a grandmother shaping yet another generation through love, wisdom, prayer, and quiet strength.

Much of what fills these pages was first lived long before it was ever written — through her tears, her prayers, her sacrifices, her perseverance, and her unwavering faith in God through every season.

While many see the visible fruit today, only Heaven fully knows the countless silent battles she fought for her children and family behind closed doors.

The greatest sermons are not always preached from pulpits; some are lived faithfully inside homes.

This book stands as a testimony that a mother's prayer never falls to the ground.

PREFACE

A Mother's Prayer: The Hidden Power That Shapes Generations

There are prayers that move mountains.
There are prayers that change nations.
And then there are prayers whispered quietly by mothers — prayers that Heaven hears with unusual attention.

This book was born from the deep conviction that some of the greatest spiritual battles in history were fought not on platforms, battlefields, or palaces, but in hidden rooms where mothers knelt beside beds, cried through sleepless nights, and carried generations before God.

Many of the world's most influential lives were shaped long before public success appeared. Behind prophets, leaders, reformers, pastors, missionaries, and history-makers, there was often a praying mother who refused to surrender her family to darkness.

- ✓ *Before Samuel became a prophet, Hannah travailed in prayer.*
- ✓ *Before Moses delivered Israel, Jochebed protected him through courageous faith.*
- ✓ *Before Jesus began His earthly ministry, Mary surrendered herself completely to God's purpose.*
- ✓ *Before Timothy became a spiritual leader, faith first lived in Lois and Eunice.*

Scripture repeatedly reveals a profound truth:
God works through praying mothers to shape generations.

Yet society often underestimates motherhood. The world measures success by titles, wealth, influence, and visibility. But Heaven measures differently. Heaven sees hidden sacrifices, silent tears, whispered prayers, exhausted faithfulness, and unseen acts of surrender. A mother may appear ordinary externally while carrying extraordinary spiritual influence internally.

This book was not written merely to encourage mothers emotionally. It was written to awaken revelation. It was written to remind mothers that prayer reaches where parenting cannot. It was written to reveal that tears surrendered to God become seeds of transformation. It was written to show that children first grow in atmosphere before they grow in achievement. It was written to teach that a mother's spiritual influence often outlives her earthly lifetime.

And perhaps most importantly, it was written to restore hope to weary hearts.

Because many mothers today are silently carrying burdens few people fully understand.

- ✓ *Some are praying for prodigal children.*
- ✓ *Some are fighting fear over the future.*
- ✓ *Some are carrying grief, disappointment, loneliness, or emotional exhaustion.*
- ✓ *Some feel inadequate because of past mistakes.*
- ✓ *Some wonder whether their prayers still matter after years of waiting.*
- ✓ *Some are trying to build godly homes in ungodly environments.*
- ✓ *Some are exhausted from carrying families spiritually while appearing strong externally.*

To every such mother, this book carries a message:

- ✓ *Heaven has heard every whisper.*
- ✓ *God remembers every tear.*
- ✓ *Your prayers are not wasted.*
- ✓ *And what you have planted in prayer will rise in power.*

Throughout these pages, you will discover biblical truths, practical wisdom, prophetic encouragement, emotional healing, and spiritual strategies designed not only to inspire you — but to strengthen you for the journey of building generations.

This book will take you through the 7 P's of a Mother's Prayer:

Prayer, Purpose, Planning, Preparation, Perseverance, Pain, and Prophecy.

You will also walk through the hidden battles mothers face and the eternal rewards that faithful intercession produces.

Every chapter was written with the desire to make this message deeply practical, biblically anchored, emotionally healing, and easy to teach, preach, share, and apply in everyday life.

The real-life stories included are fictional, yet they reflect very real struggles, emotions, and victories experienced by countless mothers around the world.

As you read this book, my prayer is that you will not merely receive information — but transformation.

- ✓ *May discouraged mothers regain hope.*
- ✓ *May weary mothers regain strength.*
- ✓ *May wounded mothers encounter healing.*
- ✓ *May fearful mothers rediscover faith.*
- ✓ *May praying mothers realize the eternal significance of what they carry.*
- ✓ *And may generations yet unborn one day rise and call blessed the mothers who chose to pray instead of quit.*

Because a mother's prayer never falls to the ground. It echoes through Heaven. It shapes destinies. And it changes generations forever.

INTRODUCTION
Behind Every Great Life Is Often a Praying Mother

"For this child I prayed; and the Lord hath given me my petition which I asked of Him."
— 1 Samuel 1:27

There are some battles in life that intelligence cannot solve, influence cannot prevent, and money cannot heal. There are storms that enter homes silently, wounds that form deep within children unseen by society, and attacks against families that cannot merely be corrected through discipline, education, or opportunity. Some battles are spiritual before they are visible. Some victories are born in prayer long before they appear in reality.

That is why throughout history, behind many great men and women, there was often a praying mother.

Before Samuel became a prophet, Hannah travailed in prayer. Before Moses became a deliverer, Jochebed hid him with courage and faith. Before Jesus began His earthly ministry, Mary surrendered herself completely to God's purpose. Before Timothy became a spiritual son to the Apostle Paul, there were the hidden prayers and faith of Eunice and Lois shaping his foundation quietly within the walls of a home.

The world celebrates platforms, titles, achievements, and public victories. Heaven often celebrates the unseen mother who wept privately, prayed silently, sacrificed continually, and believed faithfully.

A mother's prayer is one of the greatest invisible forces on earth.

It is not merely emotional concern. It is spiritual warfare.

It is not simply affection. It is prophetic investment into destiny.

It is not weakness. It is power wrapped in tears.

Many mothers underestimate what God has placed within them. They may feel ordinary, overlooked, exhausted, or unseen. Yet Scripture repeatedly reveals that God entrusts unusual influence to mothers because mothers shape atmospheres before children shape the world.

Long before a child enters a classroom, enters a career, or enters society, that child first develops within an atmosphere created at home. Children absorb fears, faith, anger, peace, hope, words, and spiritual climate long before they understand theology. A mother often becomes the first voice, the first teacher, the first comforter, the first example of faith, and sometimes the first picture of God's love a child will ever experience.

This is why Satan attacks motherhood so fiercely.

The enemy understands something many people do not: if he can wound the mother, weaken the home, distort identity, and silence prayer, he can affect generations. The attack is often deeper than the individual woman herself. Many mothers battle discouragement, emotional exhaustion, guilt, fear, anxiety for their children, and silent tears because motherhood itself is a battlefield.

Pharaoh did not merely attack Hebrew babies in Egypt; he attacked future deliverers. Herod did not merely seek children in Bethlehem; he sought to destroy destiny. Throughout Scripture, Satan

repeatedly targets children because he fears what future generations may become under the hand of God.
But what the enemy fears most is a mother who knows how to pray.

Prayer reaches places parenting cannot.
A mother may not be able to sit beside her child in every classroom, workplace, airport, relationship, or season of life. But prayer travels where human presence cannot go. A praying mother can stand before God concerning things her eyes cannot yet see.

- ✓ *Some prayers become shields.*
- ✓ *Some become seeds.*
- ✓ *Some become spiritual walls around children.*
- ✓ *Some become prophetic declarations over futures that seem impossible.*
- ✓ *And some become generational turning points.*

Many mothers today carry pain they never speak about openly. Some pray for children trapped in addiction. Some cry over broken relationships. Some silently fear for the future of their families. Some feel they have failed. Some carry regret over past mistakes. Some wonder whether their prayers still matter after years of silence.
Yet Scripture repeatedly shows us that God works through process more often than instant answers.

- ✓ *Hannah did not receive Samuel immediately.*
- ✓ *Elizabeth waited many years before John the Baptist was born.*
- ✓ *Sarah waited through impossible seasons before Isaac arrived.*

- ✓ *Even Mary, though chosen by God, still had to walk through misunderstanding, pain, and surrender.*

One of the deepest revelations a mother must understand is this: God often prepares the mother while preparing the miracle.

Waiting seasons are not wasted seasons.

Sometimes God develops endurance before fulfillment. Sometimes He deepens faith before manifestation. Sometimes He uses tears to soften hearts that success never could.

Psalm 56:8 says, *"Put thou my tears into thy bottle: are they not in thy book?"*

Heaven does not ignore a mother's tears.

God records them.

The tears of a praying mother are never meaningless in the sight of God. What falls from a mother's eyes in prayer often rises before God as intercession. Tears become liquid seeds planted into the future.

- ✓ *There are children alive today because a mother prayed.*
- ✓ *There are marriages restored because a mother prayed.*
- ✓ *There are addictions broken because a mother prayed.*
- ✓ *There are ministries birthed because a mother refused to stop praying.*
- ✓ *There are generations preserved because one woman knelt before God and refused to give up.*

Society often underestimates mothers because it measures influence outwardly. God measures differently. Heaven sees the hidden shaping of character, values, spiritual atmosphere, and destiny.

A mother may feel she is "only raising children," while Heaven sees her shaping generations.

This truth becomes especially clear when we study Hannah in 1 Samuel.

Hannah was barren, misunderstood, and emotionally broken. She carried shame in a culture where motherhood was deeply tied to identity. Yet in the middle of her pain, she prayed one of the most powerful prayers recorded in Scripture. She did not merely ask God for personal happiness. She surrendered her future child back to God's purpose.

"For this child I prayed…"

Those words are simple, but they carry deep revelation.

Samuel was not born accidentally into destiny. He was birthed through prayer.

Before Samuel ever heard God's voice in the temple, his mother had already spoken his future into Heaven.

Before he became a prophet to nations, he first became an answer to a mother's tears.

The same pattern appears in the New Testament.

Timothy became a strong spiritual leader under the mentorship of Paul, but Paul specifically acknowledged the faith that first lived in his grandmother Lois and his mother Eunice.

"And that from a child thou hast known the holy scriptures…" — 2 Timothy 3:15

Notice that Timothy did not suddenly become spiritual as an adult. Seeds had already been planted in childhood.

Invisible foundations produce visible futures.

The world often notices greatness only after it becomes public. God notices the hidden seasons first.

One mother may shape a family.

One praying woman may alter the spiritual direction of generations.

One surrendered womb may carry future deliverers, worshippers, teachers, reformers, evangelists, and kingdom builders.

Motherhood is far more than biological responsibility. It is spiritual stewardship.

The womb itself is deeply prophetic throughout Scripture. God repeatedly used wombs connected to impossibility, surrender, prayer, or divine intervention to birth individuals who carried unusual assignments.

Samuel.

Isaac.

John the Baptist.

Jesus.

None of them entered the earth casually.

Heaven had purpose attached to their arrival.

This means motherhood must never be reduced merely to daily routine, cooking, cleaning, schedules, or survival. Though those responsibilities are sacred, there is something even deeper happening spiritually. Every praying mother is building invisible foundations beneath visible lives.

The tragedy today is that many mothers prepare children academically, socially, financially, and professionally, yet neglect spiritual preparation. But success without spiritual foundation often collapses under pressure.

A child can be educated and still be empty. Talented and still broken. Successful and still lost. This is why prayer matters.

- ✓ *Prayer builds what money cannot buy.*
- ✓ *Prayer reaches where lectures cannot reach.*
- ✓ *Prayer protects when mothers cannot physically be present.*
- ✓ *Prayer keeps spiritual doors open even when children wander temporarily.*

Some mothers reading these pages may feel discouraged because their children are far from God today. Perhaps rebellion has entered the home. Perhaps communication has broken down. Perhaps years of effort seem wasted.

But this book carries a message of hope:

- ✓ *A mother's prayer outlives seasons.*
- ✓ *Seeds planted in tears do not die easily.*
- ✓ *God can still reach wandering children.*
- ✓ *Prodigals can still come home.*
- ✓ *Generational destruction can still be reversed.*

No matter how dark the situation appears, Luke 1:37 still declares:

"For with God nothing shall be impossible."

The purpose of this book is not merely to encourage mothers emotionally for a moment. It is to awaken them spiritually to the power Heaven has entrusted to them.

This book will reveal that:

- ✓ *Mothers shape invisible foundations.*
- ✓ *Prayer reaches where parenting cannot.*
- ✓ *Tears become seeds before God.*
- ✓ *A praying mother can reverse generational destruction.*
- ✓ *God often answers through process, not instant miracles.*

A mother's prayer can outlive her lifetime.

Many years ago, a woman named Grace sat awake night after night praying for her son Daniel. As a teenager, Daniel had become rebellious, angry, and distant from God. He began drinking heavily, abandoned church completely, and eventually moved overseas. Grace often cried silently after phone calls with him because each conversation seemed colder than the last.

Friends told her to "accept reality." Some even suggested she had failed as a mother.

But Grace continued praying.

Every morning before sunrise, she sat at her dining table with an old Bible, praying over Daniel's life. Sometimes she had no words left. Sometimes only tears fell onto the pages of Scripture. Yet she continued declaring God's promises over her son.

Years passed.

Nothing appeared to change.

Then one evening Daniel entered a small church overseas simply to escape a storm outside. During the service, something broke within him. He wept uncontrollably and surrendered his life to Christ.

Years later, Daniel became a missionary helping troubled young men recover from addiction and violence.

At a conference one day, someone asked him, "What brought you back to God?"

Daniel paused before answering.

"My mother's prayers followed me farther than I could run."

That is the power of a praying mother.

Long after words are forgotten…

Long after children grow older…

Long after seasons change…
A mother's prayers continue speaking before God.
And often, behind every transformed life, healed family, restored child, or changed generation…
there is still a praying mother kneeling somewhere in the shadows.

Reflection Questions

- ✓ *What spiritual atmosphere currently exists within my home?*
- ✓ *What words do my children hear most often from me?*
- ✓ *Am I preparing my children spiritually or only academically?*
- ✓ *What fears about my children do I need to surrender to God?*
- ✓ *Have I allowed discouragement to silence my prayers?*
- ✓ *What generational patterns need to be broken through prayer in my family?*

Practical Action Plan

Step 1: Create a Prayer Atmosphere
Choose one consistent place and time daily to pray over your children, even if only for fifteen minutes.

Step 2: Speak Life Intentionally
Begin declaring Scripture over your children instead of speaking fear, frustration, or negativity.

Step 3: Build Spiritual Foundations Early
Introduce simple spiritual habits at home: worship, prayer, Scripture reading, gratitude, and blessing conversations.

Family Exercise
As a family, write down three prayers or dreams for your household and place them in a visible location. Spend one evening each week praying together over them.

Declaration
"I will not fear for my children's future. My prayers are building foundations Heaven recognizes. My tears are not wasted. God is working even when I cannot yet see the results."

Prayer for Mothers
Heavenly Father,
Strengthen every weary mother reading these pages. Heal every hidden wound, every silent fear, and every disappointment carried in secret. Remind her that her prayers matter, her tears are seen, and her labor is not in vain.
Teach her to build spiritually, speak prophetically, and trust You completely with her children's future. Protect her home from every attack of darkness. Restore broken relationships. Bring prodigal children back to You. Raise up godly generations from her household.
May every mother discover that prayer is not her last option—it is her greatest weapon.
In Jesus' name, Amen.

PART 1

THE 7 P's OF A MOTHER'S PRAYER

CHAPTER 1
PRAYER
"For This Child I Prayed"

"For this child I prayed; and the Lord hath given me my petition which I asked of Him."
— 1 Samuel 1:27

There are some things in life that cannot be built by human strength alone. Some destinies are too fragile to survive without prayer. Some battles are too invisible for ordinary methods. Some children carry assignments from God that will attract spiritual opposition long before greatness appears outwardly. This is why one of the greatest gifts a mother can give her child is not merely education, opportunity, wealth, or protection—but prayer.

Prayer is spiritual planting before physical harvest.

Every praying mother must understand this revelation deeply: prayer is never empty activity. Whenever a mother kneels before God concerning her child, she is planting something into the unseen realm that will eventually affect the visible world. Seeds placed into the soil disappear before they emerge. In the same way, many prayers seem invisible before they become visible answers.

One of the painful realities of motherhood is that mothers often pray long before they see results. They pray when children are asleep. They pray through tears no one sees. They pray through fear, uncertainty, disappointment, rebellion, silence, and

waiting. Sometimes they even pray while wondering whether Heaven is listening.
Yet Scripture repeatedly reveals that some of the greatest miracles in history were first born through persistent prayer.

Hannah is one of the clearest examples.
When we first meet Hannah in 1 Samuel, we do not see celebration—we see pain. She carried the agony of barrenness in a culture where a woman's identity was often tied to motherhood. Year after year she endured misunderstanding, shame, and emotional torment. Others around her could not fully understand her private sorrow.
But pain pushed Hannah toward prayer instead of bitterness.
That decision changed history.
In 1 Samuel 1, Hannah entered the temple carrying deep anguish within her soul. The Bible says she prayed unto the Lord and "wept sore." These were not polished religious words. They were broken cries from a wounded heart. Even Eli the priest misunderstood her intensity and assumed she was drunk.
But Heaven understood.
One of the greatest lessons mothers must learn is this: God understands prayers that people misinterpret.
Some prayers never sound impressive publicly. Some are whispered through tears. Some are spoken while driving children to school. Some are prayed silently beside hospital beds. Some are released through exhaustion late at night after everyone else is asleep.
Yet Heaven hears every one of them.

Hannah's prayer was powerful not merely because she wanted a child, but because she surrendered the child back to God. Her prayer was not selfish ambition; it was spiritual surrender.

"And I will give him unto the Lord all the days of his life…" — 1 Samuel 1:11

This is where prayer becomes transformative. True prayer does not merely ask God to bless our plans; it surrenders our children to His purpose.

Many parents today pray mainly for success, safety, education, careers, or financial stability for their children. While those things are important, heaven sees deeper. God is concerned not merely with what children achieve but with who they become.

- ✓ *A child can be successful and still spiritually empty.*
- ✓ *A child can be wealthy yet broken.*
- ✓ *A child can become admired publicly while privately lost.*

This is why mothers must pray beyond temporary achievements. Prayer must touch destiny.

Hannah understood something profound: children are not possessions to control; they are assignments to steward.

Samuel did not belong only to Hannah. He belonged to God's purpose.

And because Hannah prayed, a prophet was raised who would eventually shape an entire nation.

The spiritual condition of Israel was dark during Samuel's birth. Corruption existed in leadership. Spiritual decline had spread across the land. Yet while the nation focused on visible problems, God was preparing an answer through the womb and prayers of one woman.

Never underestimate what God can birth through a praying mother.
Sometimes Heaven's answer to a generation begins in hidden prayer.
Throughout Scripture, God repeatedly reveals this pattern.
Before Moses delivered Israel, Jochebed protected him through courage and faith. Pharaoh issued commands to destroy Hebrew sons, but one mother refused to surrender her child to fear. While Egypt saw another Hebrew baby, Heaven saw a deliverer.
Before Jesus entered public ministry, Mary first surrendered herself to the impossible promise of God.
"Be it unto me according to thy word." — Luke 1:38
Mary teaches us that prayer is not only asking God for things—it is yielding ourselves to God's process.
There are moments when mothers will not understand the full future of their children. Mary certainly did not fully comprehend everything Jesus would face. Simeon even warned her that sorrow would pierce her own soul.
Yet she continued trusting God.
Real prayer often requires surrender before understanding.
Even Jesus Himself demonstrated the power of intercessory prayer over people He loved. Before Peter's greatest failure, Jesus told him:
"But I have prayed for thee, that thy faith fail not…" — Luke 22:32
Notice carefully: Jesus did not say Peter would never struggle. He did not say Peter would never fail temporarily. Instead, He prayed that Peter's faith would survive the attack.
This is deeply important for mothers to understand.

Sometimes prayer does not prevent struggle immediately; it preserves destiny through the struggle.

Many mothers become discouraged when children wander temporarily. They assume failure means the prayers did not work. But some prayers continue working beneath the surface long after visible rebellion appears.

Peter fell—but he did not remain fallen.

Why? Because prayer had already gone ahead of him.

A praying mother must learn that prayer reaches places her physical presence cannot go.

A mother cannot stand beside her child every moment of life. She cannot enter every classroom, friendship, relationship, workplace, airport, university, or private conversation. But prayer travels beyond distance.

Prayer enters places where human hands cannot reach.

Some mothers are carrying heavy burdens today because they feel powerless concerning their children. Perhaps a son has become distant. Perhaps a daughter is emotionally wounded. Perhaps addiction, wrong influences, bitterness, or rebellion have entered the picture.

But prayer is often strongest precisely when mothers feel weakest.

James 5:16 declares: *"The effectual fervent prayer of a righteous man availeth much."*

Prayer is not passive weakness. It is spiritual authority.

- ✓ *One praying mother can alter atmospheres within a home.*

- ✓ *One praying mother can break cycles that affected generations.*
- ✓ *One praying mother can release peace into chaos.*
- ✓ *One praying mother can build invisible spiritual walls around her children.*
- ✓ *One praying mother can plant seeds that bloom years later.*

Sometimes mothers expect immediate results from prayer and become discouraged when answers delay. But many of God's answers unfold through process rather than instant manifestation.

Seeds do not become harvest overnight.

Pregnancy itself teaches this principle. Growth happens invisibly before it becomes visible. In the same way, many prayers are working underground before mothers see outward evidence.

Jeremiah 33:3 says: *"Call unto me, and I will answer thee, and show thee great and mighty things, which thou knowest not."*

Notice that God did not promise instant answers only. Sometimes He reveals things progressively. Prayer develops spiritual sensitivity. Praying mothers begin discerning dangers, opportunities, burdens, and directions that natural wisdom alone cannot provide.

Prayer sharpens discernment.

There are moments when mothers will sense something is wrong long before visible evidence appears. There are times God burdens mothers spiritually concerning situations unfolding in the future. Many mothers later realize that prayer became divine preparation before crisis arrived.

Prayer is not merely conversation with God—it is partnership with Him.

One of the most remarkable historical examples outside Scripture is Monica, the mother of Augustine. Augustine lived rebelliously for years, pursuing sinful lifestyles and rejecting godly influence despite Monica's continual prayers.

Many people would have given up.

But Monica continued interceding faithfully for her son. She prayed through disappointment, heartbreak, and delay. Her tears became seeds before God.

Eventually Augustine surrendered his life to Christ and later became one of the most influential Christian thinkers in history.

Behind Augustine's transformation stood the hidden prayers of a mother who refused to stop believing.

The world often celebrates transformed people while overlooking the intercession that preceded the transformation.

A mother's prayer may become the unseen reason future generations encounter God.

Many years ago, a woman named Rebecca faced the crushing pain of infertility. Month after month she battled disappointment while watching others celebrate pregnancies around her. Church became emotionally difficult because every baby dedication reminded her of her own longing.

Though she smiled publicly, privately she often wept.

There were seasons when she questioned whether God had forgotten her entirely.

But instead of allowing pain to harden her heart, Rebecca began praying differently. She stopped praying only for a child and started praying for purpose.

"Lord," she would whisper, "if You bless me with a child, let this life belong to You."

Years later, Rebecca gave birth to a son named Caleb.

But the deeper miracle was not merely the birth itself—it was what prayer built within her during the waiting years. Infertility had taught her surrender, dependence, compassion, and spiritual depth. She later became a source of healing and encouragement to many hurting women facing similar struggles.

Sometimes the greatest miracle is not merely the answer God gives but the person we become while waiting.

This is one of the hidden powers of prayer. Prayer changes mothers before it changes circumstances.

A praying mother becomes spiritually stronger, emotionally deeper, and more discerning over time. Prayer teaches dependence on God rather than control over outcomes.

And perhaps one of the greatest revelations in this chapter is this:

Children may forget many conversations, but they rarely escape the atmosphere created by a praying mother.

Children remember hearing whispered prayers from another room.

- ✓ *They remember mothers laying hands on them before school.*
- ✓ *They remember tears during worship.*
- ✓ *They remember Scripture spoken during difficult seasons.*
- ✓ *They remember peace during storms.*

- ✓ *Even when children wander temporarily, those memories remain planted deeply within them.*

Prayer leaves spiritual fingerprints on lives.
Many adults who later return to God often trace their journey back to the prayers of a mother or grandmother. The prayers may not have produced immediate visible change, but they remained alive beneath the surface.

A mother's prayer often outlives her lifetime.

Some women reading these pages may feel tired. Perhaps you have prayed for years without visible answers. Perhaps disappointment has tempted you to stop believing.

But do not underestimate what God is doing invisibly.

Heaven specializes in hidden growth.

Roots develop before fruit appears.

- ✓ *Continue praying.*
- ✓ *Continue declaring God's promises.*
- ✓ *Continue building spiritual foundations.*
- ✓ *Continue planting seeds in tears if necessary.*

Galatians 6:9 reminds us: *"And let us not be weary in well doing: for in due season we shall reap, if we faint not."*

Due season still exists.

And sometimes the greatest miracles are already growing underground while mothers are still praying above the surface.

How to Pray Over Your Children

Praying over children should move beyond routine repetition. Prayer becomes powerful when it is intentional, Scripture-based, future-focused, and spiritually specific.

- ✓ *Pray for their salvation before success.*

- ✓ *Pray for character before comfort.*
- ✓ *Pray for wisdom before popularity.*
- ✓ *Pray for spiritual discernment before achievement.*
- ✓ *Pray for future friendships, future spouses, future decisions, future protection, and future purpose.*

Instead of praying only against problems, begin praying toward destiny.

Do not pray merely from fear. Pray from faith.

Daily Declarations Over Children

- ✓ *"Lord, my children shall walk in wisdom and truth."*
- ✓ *"They will not be destroyed by the pressures of this world."*
- ✓ *"They will fulfill the purpose of God for their lives."*
- ✓ *"They will hear Your voice clearly."*
- ✓ *"No weapon formed against them shall prosper."*
- ✓ *"They will become carriers of peace, integrity, and godliness."*

Reflection Questions

- ✓ *What fears concerning my children have been greater than my faith?*
- ✓ *Have I prayed more about behavior or about destiny?*
- ✓ *What spiritual atmosphere am I creating within my home?*
- ✓ *Do my children hear words of blessing or constant criticism?*
- ✓ *Have delays in answered prayer discouraged my faith?*

Practical Action Plan

Step 1: Create a Prayer Journal

Write specific prayers, promises, burdens, and Scriptures concerning each child. Record answered prayers to strengthen faith during waiting seasons.

Step 2: Build a Prayer Space

Create a consistent place where you meet God daily. It need not be large or impressive. What matters is consistency and surrender.

Step 3: Pray Scripture Daily

Turn Bible verses into personal prayers over your children's lives.

Family Exercise

Gather as a family once a week and allow each member to pray for another member specifically. Teach children early that prayer is normal, powerful, and personal.

Declaration

"My prayers are planting seeds into my children's future. Heaven hears every cry, records every tear, and works beyond what I can presently see. My children belong to God's purpose, and no attack of darkness will destroy their destiny."

Prayer for Mothers

Heavenly Father,

Teach me to pray with faith and perseverance. When I grow weary, strengthen me. When fear rises, remind me that You love my children even more than I do. Help me to build spiritually and not merely naturally. Let my home become an atmosphere of peace, worship, truth, and prayer.

Protect my children from dangers seen and unseen. Draw prodigal hearts back to You. Heal wounds hidden deep within them. Surround them with godly influences and wise relationships.

And Lord, let the seeds I plant in prayer today become testimonies tomorrow.

In Jesus' name, Amen.

CHAPTER 2
PURPOSE
"Children Are More Than Achievements"

"Before I formed thee in the belly I knew thee..."
— Jeremiah 1:5

One of the greatest mistakes modern parenting makes is reducing children to achievements instead of recognizing them as assignments from God.

Society measures children by marks, medals, careers, salaries, appearances, and accomplishments. Parents often feel pressured to raise children who are successful in the eyes of the world. Conversations become centered around performance, education, rankings, admissions, careers, and social approval.

But Heaven asks a different question.

Not merely, *"Will this child succeed?"*

But, *"Will this child fulfill purpose?"*

There is a profound difference between success and purpose. A person can achieve public success and still miss divine assignment. A child may become wealthy, admired, influential, and educated while remaining disconnected from the very reason they were created.

God never creates human life accidentally.

Every child enters the earth carrying purpose. Every birth carries possibility. Every child is born with seeds of destiny hidden within them.

This is why motherhood must go beyond raising accomplished children. Mothers are called to discern, nurture, protect, and guide purpose.

Jeremiah 1:5 reveals one of the deepest truths in Scripture:
"Before I formed thee in the belly I knew thee…"
Notice carefully—God speaks of knowing Jeremiah before formation. Before physical development began, purpose already existed in the mind of God.
This means children do not discover purpose after birth; they are born with it already placed within them by God.
A mother therefore becomes more than a caretaker. She becomes a steward of divine potential.
One of the greatest responsibilities of motherhood is helping children discover not merely what they can do, but who God created them to become.
This truth changes everything.
It changes how mothers pray.
It changes how they speak.
It changes how they discipline.
It changes how they encourage.
It changes how they see weakness, gifting, personality, struggles, and even delays in development.
Many children become emotionally wounded because they are constantly forced into molds they were never designed to fit. Parents often unknowingly try to reproduce themselves through their children rather than recognizing the unique calling God placed within them.

Comparison has damaged countless destinies.
Some children are naturally expressive while others are reflective. Some lead boldly while others carry deep compassion quietly. Some communicate publicly while others build faithfully behind the

scenes. Some are gifted intellectually, others creatively, spiritually, relationally, or strategically.
But modern culture tends to celebrate only certain forms of success.
This creates pressure within homes.
Children begin believing they are valuable only when they perform well enough.
Yet Scripture repeatedly shows us that God often chooses people society overlooks.
David was ignored while his brothers were presented publicly.
Moses struggled with insecurity and speech.
Joseph endured rejection before leadership.
Gideon saw himself as insignificant.
And even Jesus, according to Isaiah 53, had *"no beauty that we should desire him."*
God sees differently from man.
Heaven looks beyond outward appearance into divine assignment.
This is why mothers must learn to discern purpose beneath imperfection.
Psalm 139:16 declares: *"Thine eyes did see my substance, yet being unperfect; and in thy book all my members were written…"*
Before a child ever speaks a word, enters school, or accomplishes anything publicly, God already sees their future.
There are mothers reading these pages who are worried because their children do not seem extraordinary by worldly standards. Perhaps a child struggles academically. Perhaps another is emotionally withdrawn. Perhaps one seems slower than others socially or intellectually.
But never allow temporary weakness to blind you to eternal purpose.

Some of the greatest destinies begin hidden beneath struggle.

Samuel's story reveals this beautifully.
Israel was spiritually dark during Samuel's birth. Corruption filled leadership. The voice of God had become rare in the land. Yet Heaven was preparing an answer through a child birthed by prayer.
Samuel was not born merely to become successful personally. He was born to restore spiritual direction to a nation.
This is why Hannah's prayer mattered so deeply.
She did not merely ask for a son to remove her shame. She surrendered Samuel to God's purpose.
Many parents ask God to bless their children.
But praying mothers must also ask: *"Lord, what were they born for?"*
Children are more than emotional fulfillment for parents.
They are more than family extensions.
They are more than future providers.
They are more than achievements to display.
They are carriers of assignment.
The tragedy today is that many homes prepare children extensively for careers but neglect preparation for calling.
Children are taught how to earn money, but not how to hear God.
They are trained academically, but not spiritually.
They are prepared for competition, but not for character.
They are pushed toward ambition, but not always toward purpose.
Yet purpose is what sustains people through storms.
Careers may change.

Economies may collapse.
Platforms may disappear.
But purpose remains.

- ✓ *Purpose gives suffering meaning.*
- ✓ *Purpose gives hardship endurance.*
- ✓ *Purpose gives identity stability.*
- ✓ *Purpose anchors lives beyond temporary success.*

This truth becomes especially visible in the life of Samson.

Before Samson was born, an angel appeared declaring that the child would carry divine assignment from birth.

"For, lo, thou shalt conceive, and bear a son… and he shall begin to deliver Israel…"
— Judges 13:5

Samson's purpose existed before his birth.

Yet Samson's story also reveals a sobering truth: gifting alone is not enough.

A child can carry great purpose yet still require guidance, discipline, wisdom, and spiritual foundation. Calling without character eventually collapses.

This is why mothers must nurture not only talent, but spiritual maturity.

Many parents celebrate gifting while ignoring character development. But God is more concerned about who children become inwardly than what they achieve outwardly.

John the Baptist's life also reveals purpose-centered parenting beautifully.

Before John was born, God had already declared his assignment.

"He shall be great in the sight of the Lord…" — Luke 1:15

John's parents understood that this child belonged to something larger than personal ambition. His life carried prophetic significance.

Children flourish differently when they grow within homes that value purpose more than performance.

A child who knows they are loved only when successful becomes anxious.

A child constantly compared to others becomes insecure.

A child pressured to meet unrealistic expectations often loses confidence.

But a child nurtured according to God's design develops identity rooted deeper than achievement.

Many mothers unintentionally wound children through comparison.

Comparison is one of the quiet destroyers of purpose.

- ✓ *Why can't you be like your brother?*
- ✓ *Look at how well she performs.*
- ✓ *Other children are doing better.*

Comparison communicates rejection of identity.

God never intended children to become replicas of one another. Purpose is unique.

A mother's words therefore become deeply important.

Words shape identity long before destiny becomes visible.

Many children eventually become what they repeatedly hear spoken over them.

This is why praying mothers must become speaking mothers.

- ✓ *Speak life.*
- ✓ *Speak purpose.*
- ✓ *Speak identity.*
- ✓ *Speak possibility.*

- ✓ *Speak destiny.*

Even when current behavior appears disappointing, never speak permanently about temporary seasons.

The child struggling today may become the leader tomorrow.

The quiet child may become a powerful voice later.

The emotionally sensitive child may one day heal wounded people.

The deeply curious child may become a thinker, inventor, teacher, or reformer.

Do not interpret present weakness as permanent limitation.

Romans 8:28 reminds us: *"And we know that all things work together for good to them that love God, to them who are the called according to his purpose."*

Notice that God connects all things to purpose.

Even painful seasons can become preparation.

Even delays can develop depth.

Even struggles may shape future ministry.

Sometimes mothers become frustrated because children do not fit conventional expectations. Yet many unusual children later become extraordinary adults precisely because God designed them differently.

A woman named Lydia once struggled deeply concerning her son Ethan. Teachers constantly complained about him. He seemed distracted, overly imaginative, emotionally intense, and uninterested in traditional academic patterns. Other parents spoke proudly about high scores and awards while Lydia quietly worried something was wrong with her child.

One day, after another discouraging school meeting, Lydia sat alone crying before God.

"Lord," she prayed, "help me see my son the way You see him."

That prayer changed everything.
Instead of focusing only on Ethan's weaknesses, she began noticing his gifts. He showed unusual compassion toward hurting people. He remembered details others ignored. He spent hours drawing, creating, imagining, and helping younger children feel included.
Lydia began speaking differently over him.
Instead of calling him difficult, she called him thoughtful.
Instead of criticizing constantly, she encouraged intentionally.
Instead of comparing him, she prayed for discernment.
Years later Ethan became a counselor working with emotionally wounded teenagers. The same sensitivity once criticized became the very tool God used to heal others.
Many children do not need harsher pressure.
They need parents who discern purpose correctly.
This does not mean mothers ignore discipline or excuse sin. Purpose must still be shaped with wisdom, correction, accountability, and truth. But discipline should guide destiny, not crush identity.
Children must know:

- ✓ *"I am loved beyond performance."*
- ✓ *"I am valuable beyond achievement."*
- ✓ *"I was created intentionally."*
- ✓ *"I carry purpose."*

One of the greatest gifts a mother can give her child is helping them discover that they are known by God personally.
Children grounded in purpose become harder for the world to destroy.

Why? Because identity anchored in God withstands comparison, rejection, peer pressure, and failure more effectively.
A child who knows purpose may stumble temporarily but will often rise again because something deeper calls them forward.
This is why mothers must pray not only for protection, provision, and success—but for revelation.
"Lord, show me who this child truly is."
That prayer can transform parenting completely.
Some mothers reading this chapter may feel regret because of mistakes made in raising children. Perhaps words spoken in frustration caused wounds. Perhaps pressure replaced understanding. Perhaps comparison damaged confidence.
But God restores.
He heals relationships.
He renews identity.
He redeems broken seasons.
And He can still reveal purpose even after painful years.
No child is beyond God's ability to restore direction.
No destiny is too damaged for grace.
And no mother is disqualified because she was imperfect.
Throughout Scripture, God consistently works through imperfect families and imperfect people.
Yet purpose still prevails when surrendered to Him.
The greatest prayer mothers can pray is not merely:
"Lord, make my child successful."
But: *"Lord, let my child become everything You created them to be."*
That prayer changes generations.

Discovering Spiritual Gifting in Children

Children often reveal purpose through natural tendencies long before adulthood.

- ✓ *Some show leadership early.*
- ✓ *Some display compassion.*
- ✓ *Some communicate deeply.*
- ✓ *Some build, organize, protect, create, teach, or encourage naturally.*

Parents must observe prayerfully rather than forcefully controlling identity.

Purpose usually leaves clues.

Speaking Destiny Over Children

Words become spiritual atmosphere within homes.

Children who constantly hear criticism often shrink emotionally.

Children who hear life spoken over them begin developing confidence rooted in identity.

Say things like:

"God has a purpose for your life."

"You are deeply loved."

"You were created intentionally."

"Your future is not an accident."

"God will use your life powerfully."

Reflection Questions

- ✓ *Am I preparing my child more for career than for calling?*
- ✓ *Have I unknowingly compared my child to others?*
- ✓ *What unique qualities has God placed within my child?*
- ✓ *Do my words build identity or create insecurity?*

- ✓ *Have I prayed for discernment concerning my child's purpose?*

Practical Action Plan

Step 1: Observe Your Child Prayerfully

Spend intentional time noticing natural gifts, burdens, personality traits, and emotional tendencies.

Step 2: Speak Life Daily

Replace criticism-driven language with identity-building words rooted in truth and grace.

Step 3: Pray for Revelation

Ask God regularly to reveal your child's assignment, strengths, weaknesses, and future direction.

Family Exercise

Set aside one evening where every family member speaks encouraging truths over another person in the home. Create an atmosphere where identity is strengthened through words.

Declaration

"My children are not accidents. They are created intentionally by God for divine purpose. I will not compare them, crush them, or define them by temporary weakness. I will nurture destiny, speak life, and partner with God in shaping generations."

Prayer for Purpose

Heavenly Father,

Help me see my children through Your eyes and not merely through human expectations. Teach me to recognize purpose beneath weakness, gifting beneath struggle, and destiny beneath imperfection.

Forgive me for moments when comparison, pressure, or fear shaped my parenting more than

faith. Give me wisdom to nurture identity carefully and lovingly.
Reveal the calling placed upon my children's lives. Protect them from confusion, insecurity, wrong influences, and misplaced identity. Let them grow into everything You designed them to become.
May my words strengthen purpose and not damage it. And may my home become a place where destiny is discovered, nurtured, and released.
In Jesus' name, Amen.

CHAPTER 3
PLANNING
"Building Beyond Today"

"Train up a child in the way he should go: and when he is old, he will not depart from it."
— Proverbs 22:6

There is a difference between raising children and building lives.

Many parents feed children, educate them, clothe them, protect them, and provide opportunities for them. All these things are important and necessary. But biblical parenting goes deeper than meeting temporary needs. Godly parenting is not merely about managing daily responsibilities; it is about intentionally building foundations that will still stand decades later.

Children do not accidentally become spiritually strong.

Character does not develop randomly.

Faith does not grow automatically.

Homes do not become spiritually healthy by chance.

Strong generations are built intentionally.

One of the greatest tragedies of modern society is that many people plan carefully for careers, finances, businesses, weddings, vacations, and retirement, yet give little intentional thought to building the spiritual culture of their homes.

Many homes operate without vision.

Without direction.

Without spiritual structure.

Without intentional atmosphere.

As a result, children are often shaped more by culture than by conviction.
But Scripture repeatedly reveals that God works through intentional builders.
Noah built intentionally.
Nehemiah rebuilt intentionally.
Moses constructed the tabernacle intentionally.
Jesus said wise builders construct their houses upon rock intentionally.
And mothers are among the greatest builders God created.
A mother may not always see immediate results, but every conversation, every atmosphere, every habit, every prayer, every boundary, every response, and every routine is quietly laying bricks into the future lives of children.
Some mothers are building accidentally.
Others are building prophetically.
The difference matters greatly.
Proverbs 22:6 says: "Train up a child in the way he should go…"
Notice that Scripture uses the word "train."

- ✓ *Training implies process.*
- ✓ *It implies consistency.*
- ✓ *It implies planning.*
- ✓ *It implies intentionality.*

Training is not occasional inspiration.
Training requires repetition, patience, structure, correction, and vision.
Many parents hope children will become godly while building homes centered entirely around entertainment, distraction, pressure, achievement, and busyness. But children become what they consistently experience.
Atmosphere shapes appetite.

What fills a home repeatedly eventually shapes the hearts within it.

This is why mothers must become intentional architects of spiritual environment.

Children are always learning, even when nobody is formally teaching.

- ✓ *They learn from tone.*
- ✓ *They learn from reactions.*
- ✓ *They learn from priorities.*
- ✓ *They learn from conflict.*
- ✓ *They learn from what parents celebrate, tolerate, ignore, and pursue.*
- ✓ *They learn from how mothers respond under pressure.*

Some of the deepest lessons children absorb are never spoken directly.

- ✓ *A child raised in constant anger often develops insecurity.*
- ✓ *A child raised in peace often learns emotional stability.*
- ✓ *A child raised around prayer learns dependence upon God naturally.*
- ✓ *A child raised around gratitude develops contentment.*
- ✓ *A child raised around criticism may eventually struggle with identity.*

Homes preach sermons long before pulpits do.

This is why planning matters spiritually.

Habakkuk 2:2 declares: *"Write the vision, and make it plain…"*

Though the verse primarily concerns prophetic vision, the principle remains powerful: what is intentional becomes clearer and stronger.

Families without vision drift.

Homes without direction become vulnerable to outside influence.

Children without intentional guidance are often discipled by culture instead of truth.

Modern culture is aggressively shaping children every day through media, entertainment, education systems, social platforms, peer influence, and digital environments. If parents do not intentionally build spiritual foundations, something else will shape them instead.

Silence itself becomes a teacher.

Passivity becomes influence.

The world never stops discipling children.

This is why intentional parenting matters more now than ever before.

Hannah understood intentional building.

When many people read Hannah's story, they focus primarily on her prayer for Samuel. But Hannah did more than pray—she planned.

She saw beyond childhood into destiny.

After Samuel's birth, Hannah did not merely celebrate emotionally. She carefully prepared for his future relationship with God.

In 1 Samuel 1:22, Hannah declared: *"I will bring him, that he may appear before the Lord, and there abide forever."*

Notice her language carefully.

She was not simply planning for Samuel's survival.

She was planning for Samuel's spiritual future.

Many parents prepare children academically while neglecting spiritual preparation. They invest heavily into tuition, activities, opportunities, technology, and appearance, yet spend little time intentionally shaping spiritual hunger, character, discernment, prayer, and biblical identity.

But Hannah understood something deeply important: Children belong not merely to our care but to God's purpose.
Samuel's future did not happen accidentally.
It was built intentionally.
The same truth appears in the life of Jochebed, the mother of Moses.
Pharaoh had issued a terrifying decree to destroy Hebrew sons. Fear filled the land. Yet Jochebed refused to surrender her child to destruction passively.
Hebrews 11:23 says:
"By faith Moses, when he was born, was hid three months of his parents…"
Jochebed did not simply panic emotionally.

- ✓ *She acted strategically.*
- ✓ *She planned.*
- ✓ *She protected.*
- ✓ *She discerned.*
- ✓ *She prepared.*

When she placed Moses into the basket upon the Nile River, this was not abandonment—it was courageous surrender mixed with wisdom.
Some mothers today feel powerless concerning the world their children are growing up in. The dangers seem overwhelming. Culture changes rapidly. Moral confusion increases. Peer pressure intensifies. Digital influence invades homes daily.
But mothers must remember this truth:
God never calls mothers merely to fear culture. He calls them to build stronger foundations.
Children who are spiritually rooted may still face storms, but roots help trees survive violent winds.
One of the greatest gifts a mother can give her child is a spiritually stable environment.

Not a perfect environment.
But a spiritually intentional one.
Children do not require flawless parents to thrive spiritually. They require authentic environments where God is honored consistently.
Many mothers feel inadequate because they compare themselves to unrealistic standards. Social media often creates pressure to become perfect mothers with perfect homes, perfect routines, perfect children, and perfect appearances.
But spiritual strength is not built through perfection.
It is built through consistency.
A child who regularly hears prayer develops familiarity with God.
A child who sees parents repent learns humility.
A child raised in worship learns reverence.
A child who watches forgiveness modeled learns grace.
Small repeated moments shape lives more than occasional dramatic events.
This is why family routines matter deeply.
Many mothers underestimate the power of ordinary spiritual habits.
Simple moments become seeds.

- ✓ *Reading Scripture together.*
- ✓ *Praying before school.*
- ✓ *Blessing children before bedtime.*
- ✓ *Discussing God naturally during meals.*
- ✓ *Worship playing within the home.*
- ✓ *Speaking peace during stressful seasons.*

These moments appear small but build invisible foundations over time.
Deuteronomy 6 reveals God's heart concerning spiritual atmosphere within families:

"And these words… shall be in thine heart: And thou shalt teach them diligently unto thy children…"
Notice the emphasis on diligence.
Spiritual influence requires intentional repetition.
Modern homes often become emotionally crowded but spiritually empty. Families may spend hours together physically while remaining disconnected spiritually.
Children today are surrounded by information but starving for wisdom.
Entertained constantly but often emotionally anxious.
Connected digitally yet isolated relationally.
This is why mothers must become guardians of atmosphere.
The spiritual climate of a home matters deeply.
Every home carries an atmosphere.
Some homes feel peaceful.
Some feel tense.
Some feel joyful.
Some feel chaotic.
Some feel emotionally safe.
Others feel emotionally exhausting.
Children absorb atmosphere long before they understand doctrine.
A mother therefore becomes one of the primary emotional and spiritual gatekeepers within the home.
This does not mean mothers carry all responsibility alone. Fathers matter deeply too. But mothers often shape daily emotional rhythm more consistently through presence, tone, nurture, and spiritual sensitivity.
A woman named Deborah realized this during one difficult season in her family. Her home had become constantly noisy, distracted, and emotionally disconnected. Everyone was busy. Devices

dominated attention. Meals were rushed. Conversations became shallow. Though the family attended church regularly, spiritual connection inside the home was weak.

One evening Deborah noticed something alarming. Her teenage daughter seemed emotionally distant, anxious, and constantly dependent on social validation online. Her younger son had become increasingly angry and impatient.

Deborah suddenly realized something important:

Her family had structure but little spiritual atmosphere.

That realization changed her approach completely.

Instead of trying to create dramatic changes overnight, she began introducing small intentional routines.

She started praying aloud briefly before school each morning.

Worship music quietly filled the home during evenings.

One night each week became family prayer and conversation time.

Phones were set aside during meals.

Instead of criticizing constantly, Deborah intentionally spoke blessing and encouragement over her children.

At first the changes felt awkward.

But over time, the atmosphere shifted.

Conversations deepened.

Peace increased.

Emotional walls softened.

Years later her daughter admitted:

"Mom, I think those small moments saved our family."

Never underestimate small intentional acts repeated consistently.

Planning spiritually does not require expensive programs or complicated systems. It requires vision.

Godly mothers build beyond today.

They understand that what happens privately now may shape public outcomes years later.

This also means mothers must evaluate influences carefully.

Many parents monitor grades carefully while ignoring influences shaping identity daily.

- ✓ *Who speaks into your child's heart?*
- ✓ *What voices dominate their thinking?*
- ✓ *What entertainment normalizes ungodliness?*
- ✓ *What relationships weaken conviction?*
- ✓ *What social media content shapes insecurity, comparison, lust, fear, or confusion?*

Children become vulnerable when homes fail to evaluate influence intentionally.

Not every open door should remain open.

Discernment is an act of love.

Protection is not control—it is stewardship.

This becomes especially important because children today are growing within one of the loudest cultures in history. Endless voices compete for attention and identity formation.

If mothers do not intentionally establish spiritual direction, culture will establish it instead.

But mothers who build intentionally create strong internal foundations within children.

And foundations matter most when storms arrive.

Jesus said in Matthew 7 that storms come against both houses—the wise builder's house and the foolish builder's house. The difference was not the existence of storms but the strength of foundations.

Wise builders think ahead.
Wise mothers build ahead.
They understand that future battles are often won through present preparation.
One of the deepest revelations in parenting is this:
Children rarely drift accidentally toward godliness.
Spiritual strength grows intentionally.
This is why praying mothers must also become planning mothers.
Prayer invites Heaven's power.
Planning creates earthly structure for that power to grow within the home.
The two must work together.
Some mothers reading this chapter may feel overwhelmed because they recognize areas needing change within their homes. But do not allow guilt to silence growth.
Transformation begins with awareness.
Small intentional changes can redirect entire generations.
No home changes overnight.
Even spiritual rebuilding happens brick by brick.
Nehemiah rebuilt walls section by section.
Godly homes are rebuilt the same way.
One prayer at a time.
One conversation at a time.
One act of consistency at a time.
One atmosphere shift at a time.
And over time, what seemed ordinary becomes deeply transformative.
Years later children may not remember every sermon they heard.
But they will remember the atmosphere they lived in.
They will remember peace.
They will remember prayer.

They will remember safety.
They will remember consistency.
They will remember mothers who built intentionally beyond today.

Building a Family Altar

A family altar is not about religious performance. It is about creating consistent spiritual connection within the home.

This may include:

- ✓ *Short daily prayer times*
- ✓ *Reading Scripture together*
- ✓ *Worship moments*
- ✓ *Family gratitude conversations*
- ✓ *Blessing children before sleep*

Consistency matters more than length.

Evaluating Spiritual Environment

Ask yourself:

- ✓ *What atmosphere dominates our home most often?*
- ✓ *Is peace present consistently?*
- ✓ *Are our conversations life-giving?*
- ✓ *What influences shape my children daily?*
- ✓ *Is God naturally included within family life?*

Evaluating Media & Influences

Parents must intentionally discern:

- ✓ *What children watch repeatedly*
- ✓ *What values entertainment promotes*
- ✓ *Which friendships strengthen or weaken character*
- ✓ *Whether technology builds connection or isolation*

Discernment protects destiny.

Reflection Questions

- ✓ *What atmosphere currently exists within my home?*
- ✓ *Am I building intentionally or reacting constantly?*
- ✓ *What routines shape my children spiritually?*
- ✓ *What voices influence my children most strongly?*
- ✓ *Are my children being discipled more by culture or by conviction?*

Practical Action Plan

Step 1: Create One Spiritual Routine

Begin with one simple consistent family spiritual habit each day.

Step 2: Evaluate Home Atmosphere

Identify emotional patterns, distractions, tensions, or unhealthy influences affecting your home.

Step 3: Build With Vision

Pray intentionally about the kind of adults you want your children to become spiritually, emotionally, and morally.

Family Exercise

Choose one evening each week as "Family Foundation Night." Spend time praying together, discussing one Scripture, sharing gratitude, and speaking encouragement over one another.

Declaration

"My home will not drift without direction. I am building intentionally through prayer, wisdom, consistency, and spiritual vision. My children will grow upon strong foundations that withstand the storms of life."

Prayer for the Home

Heavenly Father,

Teach me to build my home intentionally and wisely. Help me recognize that the small daily moments matter deeply. Give me discernment concerning every influence shaping my children's hearts and minds.

Let my home become a place of peace, truth, prayer, healing, and spiritual strength. Remove confusion, tension, fear, and unhealthy patterns. Restore broken communication and deepen love within our family.

Help me build beyond today. Give me vision to raise children who not only succeed outwardly but remain rooted spiritually.

May the atmosphere of my home honor You and strengthen generations yet to come.

In Jesus' name, Amen.

CHAPTER 4
PREPARATION
"Stitching the Coat Before the Season Arrives"

"Moreover his mother made him a little coat, and brought it to him from year to year..."
— 1 Samuel 2:19

One of the greatest acts of faith is preparation.

Faith is not merely believing God for tomorrow; it is preparing today for what God has promised tomorrow.

Many people pray for harvest while never preparing the field. They ask God for increase while remaining unprepared for responsibility. But throughout Scripture, God consistently honors people who prepare in expectation.

Noah built an ark before rain appeared.

Joseph stored grain before famine arrived.

The wise virgins carried oil before midnight came.

Preparation is faith in advance.

And few pictures of preparation are more tender, prophetic, and powerful than Hannah stitching Samuel's coat.

At first glance, 1 Samuel 2:19 appears to be a small and ordinary verse:

"Moreover his mother made him a little coat, and brought it to him from year to year..."

Yet hidden within this verse is one of the deepest revelations about motherhood in all of Scripture.

Hannah did not simply pray for Samuel's birth—she prepared continually for his growth.

Every year she stitched another coat.

Every year she made room for increase.
Every year she anticipated development.
Every year she expected Samuel to become larger, stronger, and more mature.
This is the heart of spiritual preparation.
Preparation says:
"I believe growth is coming."
"I believe God is still working."
"I believe the future matters."
"I refuse to live only for today."
Hannah's coat was not merely fabric. It was expectation sewn with faith.
Imagine Hannah carefully measuring, stitching, adjusting, and preparing that garment year after year. Samuel was no longer living in her house. He was serving in the temple under Eli. She saw him only periodically. Yet every stitch carried expectation.
Perhaps she remembered his previous size while sewing the next coat.
Perhaps she smiled through tears while preparing it.
Perhaps every thread became a silent prayer:
"Lord, let him continue growing."
This is what praying mothers do.
They prepare for growth even before growth becomes visible.
Many mothers today feel emotionally exhausted because they are constantly reacting to present problems without preparing intentionally for future seasons. But biblical parenting requires foresight.
Children are not merely surviving current stages of life—they are becoming future adults.
This changes how mothers pray.
It changes how they speak.
It changes how they discipline.

It changes how they prepare emotionally, spiritually, and relationally.

One of the greatest mistakes parents make is preparing children academically while neglecting emotional and spiritual preparation.

Children are taught mathematics but not emotional resilience.

They are trained for exams but not for temptation.

Prepared for careers but not for suffering.

Taught achievement but not discernment.

Equipped to compete but not always equipped to endure.

Yet life requires more than information.

Children need preparation for storms they have not yet encountered.

One day they will face rejection.

One day they may encounter betrayal.

One day they may battle disappointment, temptation, confusion, loneliness, pressure, heartbreak, failure, or fear.

And mothers cannot always prevent those battles.

But they can prepare children for them.

Preparation is one of the highest forms of love.

A mother who prepares spiritually is not operating from fear but from wisdom.

This truth becomes especially visible in Mary, the mother of Jesus.

Mary's assignment was unlike any other. She carried the Son of God within her womb, yet even she had to prepare through process. When the angel announced God's plan, Mary could not possibly understand the full weight of what lay ahead.

She would face misunderstanding.

Criticism.

Danger.

Pain.

And eventually, she would stand near the cross watching her son suffer.

Yet Luke 2:19 says: *"But Mary kept all these things, and pondered them in her heart."*

Mary prepared internally before public moments arrived.

She carried revelation carefully.

She developed strength privately.

She learned surrender before suffering intensified.

One of the greatest forms of preparation mothers can develop is emotional maturity.

Children are deeply affected by the emotional atmosphere surrounding them. A child raised within constant panic often develops fear. A child raised within emotional instability may struggle with security later in life.

This does not mean mothers must become emotionless or perfect. Scripture never demands perfection from mothers. But it does reveal the importance of emotional stewardship.

Prepared mothers learn how to process pain without transferring destruction.

This is important because many people raise children while still carrying unresolved wounds from their own upbringing.

Unhealed pain often leaks into parenting.

Fear becomes overprotection.

Rejection becomes control.

Anger becomes harshness.

Insecurity becomes comparison.

Bitterness becomes emotional distance.

But God desires healing not only for mothers personally but for generations flowing through them.

Sometimes preparation begins with allowing God to heal what previous generations ignored.

Lois and Eunice understood spiritual preparation deeply.

Paul told Timothy:

"When I call to remembrance the unfeigned faith that is in thee, which dwelt first in thy grandmother Lois, and thy mother Eunice…" — 2 Timothy 1:5

Notice the phrase "dwelt first."

Faith existed within the family atmosphere before it appeared publicly in Timothy's ministry.

Timothy did not suddenly become spiritually grounded accidentally.

His spiritual roots were cultivated intentionally.

Lois and Eunice prepared him long before ministry opportunities emerged.

This reveals a powerful principle:

Children often carry publicly what mothers built privately.

Some mothers become discouraged because they do not see immediate visible results from spiritual investment. But preparation often works invisibly first.

Roots grow underground before fruit appears above ground.

One of the enemy's greatest strategies against mothers is exhaustion. If mothers become overwhelmed, distracted, discouraged, emotionally wounded, or spiritually passive, intentional preparation begins to disappear. Parenting becomes survival instead of vision.

But mothers must remember:

The future is often shaped quietly within ordinary daily moments.

Small repeated actions become lifelong foundations.

A bedtime prayer repeated for years becomes spiritual memory.
A mother who apologizes after mistakes teaches humility.
A home filled with worship teaches peace.
Conversations about God during ordinary life teach children that faith is relational, not merely religious.
Preparation happens gradually.
One conversation at a time.
One correction at a time.
One prayer at a time.
One atmosphere at a time.
A woman named Rachel learned this during one of the most painful seasons of her life.
After a difficult divorce filled with conflict and betrayal, Rachel noticed troubling changes in her daughter Sophia. Once joyful and expressive, Sophia became withdrawn, fearful, and emotionally guarded. Loud arguments from the past had left invisible wounds within her young heart.
At first Rachel focused only on practical survival—work, finances, schedules, responsibilities. But one evening she overheard Sophia crying quietly in her room saying:
"Maybe families always break apart."
That sentence pierced Rachel deeply.
She suddenly realized her daughter needed more than physical provision. She needed emotional preparation and healing.
Rachel began intentionally rebuilding emotional safety within the home.
Instead of hiding pain completely, she learned to process it healthily.
She prayed openly with Sophia.
They began reading Scripture together before bed.

Rachel intentionally reassured her daughter repeatedly:
"You are safe."
"You are deeply loved."
"God will never abandon us."
Slowly Sophia began healing.
Years later, Sophia became a counselor helping children from broken homes recover emotionally.
What Rachel rebuilt intentionally in private eventually became healing for others publicly.
Prepared mothers raise resilient children.
Not because life becomes easy, but because foundations become stronger.
One of the deepest revelations in preparation is this:
Mothers are often preparing children for battles they themselves may never see.
A mother praying over a toddler may actually be preparing a future husband, wife, leader, pastor, teacher, missionary, or parent.
This is why preparation must extend beyond behavior management into character formation.

- ✓ *Teach children how to forgive.*
- ✓ *Teach them how to handle disappointment.*
- ✓ *Teach them how to pray when confused.*
- ✓ *Teach them how to stand when culture pressures compromise.*
- ✓ *Teach them how to recognize God's voice.*
- ✓ *Teach them how to process failure without losing identity.*
- ✓ *Teach them how to endure seasons when prayers seem unanswered.*

Children prepared spiritually survive storms differently.
Jesus Himself demonstrated preparation with His disciples repeatedly. Before sending them into

difficult assignments, He taught, corrected, warned, encouraged, and equipped them.

Preparation is love anticipating future need.

Many mothers want to protect children from every hardship. But God's goal is not merely fragile comfort; it is spiritual maturity.

Preparation builds endurance.

And endurance builds stability.

One of the most dangerous things parents can do is raise children externally strong but internally weak.

Children today often appear highly connected digitally yet remain emotionally fragile internally. Small disappointments crush them because they were never taught resilience, patience, or emotional endurance.

Prepared mothers teach children that storms do not mean abandonment.

Delayed answers do not mean God has failed.

Pain does not cancel purpose.

And temporary struggles do not define identity.

This is why preparation requires wisdom beyond momentary emotions.

Some mothers reading this chapter may feel regret because they recognize areas where preparation was lacking. Perhaps certain wounds were ignored. Perhaps busyness replaced intentional investment. Perhaps spiritual routines disappeared over time.

But God is gracious.

Preparation can begin again.

Nehemiah rebuilt broken walls.

God rebuilds broken foundations too.

No home is beyond restoration.

No child is beyond healing.

No mother is disqualified because she was imperfect.

God often works powerfully through surrendered mothers who are willing to grow.

And perhaps this is the deepest revelation within Hannah's little coat:

Preparation is proof that hope is still alive.

Every stitch declared expectation.

Every thread declared belief.

Every garment declared: *"I believe there is still a future."*

Some mothers today feel weary because current seasons look difficult. Perhaps children seem distant emotionally. Perhaps spiritual growth appears slow. Perhaps wounds still linger within the family.

But continue stitching the coat.

Continue preparing with faith.

Continue praying.

Continue speaking life.

Continue building emotionally healthy environments.

Continue planting seeds that may bloom later.

Because what mothers build quietly today may become strength for generations tomorrow.

Preparing Children Emotionally

Children need more than correction—they need emotional security.

Teach children:

- ✓ *How to express emotions healthily*
- ✓ *How to process disappointment*
- ✓ *How to forgive*
- ✓ *How to communicate honestly*
- ✓ *How to handle fear and anxiety through faith*

Emotionally healthy children become spiritually stronger adults.

Preparing Children Spiritually

Spiritual preparation must become part of ordinary family life.

- ✓ *Pray together naturally.*
- ✓ *Discuss Scripture practically.*
- ✓ *Model repentance sincerely.*
- ✓ *Teach children how to seek God personally, not merely attend church externally.*

Children imitate authenticity more than religious performance.

Preparing Children for Future Battles

Teach children:

- ✓ *How to resist peer pressure*
- ✓ *How to recognize unhealthy influences*
- ✓ *How to stand for truth respectfully*
- ✓ *How to endure difficulty without losing faith*
- ✓ *How to return to God after failure*

Preparation today becomes protection tomorrow.

Reflection Questions

- ✓ *Am I preparing my children only for success or also for suffering?*
- ✓ *What emotional atmosphere are my children absorbing daily?*
- ✓ *Have unresolved wounds affected my parenting?*
- ✓ *Am I building resilience or dependence?*
- ✓ *What future battles might my children need preparation for spiritually?*

Practical Action Plan

Step 1: Build Emotional Safety

Create an environment where children feel heard, valued, and secure emotionally.

Step 2: Introduce Spiritual Habits Consistently
Develop simple spiritual routines that become normal within family life.
Step 3: Prepare Beyond the Present
Pray intentionally concerning future seasons, future relationships, future temptations, and future responsibilities.

Family Exercise
Have each family member share one fear and one hope about the future. Pray together specifically over each concern and dream.

Declaration
"I will prepare my children with wisdom, prayer, emotional strength, and spiritual truth. I will not raise fragile lives without foundations. God is helping me build future-ready generations."

Prayer for Preparation
Heavenly Father,
Teach me to prepare my children wisely for the future You have planned for them. Give me discernment to recognize areas where healing, growth, and strengthening are needed.
Help me build emotional safety within my home. Heal every wound within our family that could weaken future generations. Teach me to model faith, resilience, humility, and truth consistently.
Prepare my children spiritually for every battle they may face. Guard their minds, hearts, relationships, and decisions. Give them courage to stand firm in difficult seasons and wisdom to recognize Your voice clearly.

And Lord, help me continue stitching the coat in faith—even when I cannot yet see the fullness of what You are doing.
In Jesus' name, Amen.

CHAPTER 5
PERSEVERANCE
"When Heaven Seems Silent"

"And let us not be weary in well doing: for in due season we shall reap, if we faint not."
— Galatians 6:9

One of the hardest seasons in a mother's life is not always pain itself.
It is waiting.
Waiting tests the soul differently than suffering. Pain may wound deeply, but delay often exhausts silently. There are mothers who can endure hardship bravely for a short season, yet become weary when prayers seem unanswered year after year.
Nothing stretches faith quite like silence.
Especially Heaven's silence.
There are moments when mothers pray faithfully, yet nothing appears to change. The child still struggles. The addiction continues. The rebellion remains. The emotional wounds deepen. The prodigal child stays distant. The marriage remains strained. The diagnosis persists. The fear lingers.
And quietly, deep inside, a painful question begins to rise:
"Lord… are You hearing me?"
This chapter is for every mother who has prayed through tears but still waits.
Every mother who has worshipped while wounded.
Every mother who continued believing when visible evidence disappeared.
Every mother who has carried promises while standing in painful delay.

One of the greatest revelations mothers must understand is this:
Delayed answers are not denied prayers.
God's silence is not God's absence.
And Heaven's process is often different from human expectation.
Many people think faith becomes strongest after miracles happen. But Scripture reveals that some of the deepest faith is developed before miracles arrive.
Faith matures in waiting.
Trust deepens in silence.
Character forms in delay.
And sometimes God develops the mother before delivering the miracle.
This truth appears repeatedly throughout Scripture.
Hannah's story is not merely about answered prayer—it is about enduring delay without surrendering faith.
When we first encounter Hannah in 1 Samuel, she is already wounded emotionally. Year after year she carried the agony of barrenness. And her pain was intensified because she watched others receive what she longed for desperately.
Few pains are heavier than praying for something while watching others receive it easily.
Every year Hannah went to the house of the Lord carrying hope mixed with heartbreak. Scripture tells us Peninnah provoked her "sore, for to make her fret."
The pain was not only physical barrenness—it was emotional torment.
Mockery.
Comparison.
Humiliation.
Silence.

Delay.

Yet despite years of disappointment, Hannah kept returning to God.

That is perseverance.

Perseverance is not pretending pain does not exist.

It is continuing to seek God despite pain.

Many mothers misunderstand perseverance. They think persevering means never crying, never struggling emotionally, or never feeling discouraged.

But Hannah wept.

She broke emotionally.

She poured out her soul before God.

And yet she continued praying.

This is deeply important because some mothers secretly feel guilty for feeling exhausted emotionally.

They assume strong faith means never feeling weak.

But Scripture never presents biblical heroes as emotionless people.

David cried.

Jeremiah lamented.

Job questioned.

Even Jesus wept.

Perseverance is not the absence of emotion.

It is refusing to abandon God within emotion.

Psalm 30:5 declares: *"Weeping may endure for a night, but joy cometh in the morning."*

Notice carefully—the verse does not deny weeping.

Some nights are real.

Some tears are real.

Some seasons truly hurt.

But pain is never the final chapter for those who continue trusting God.

Morning still comes.

One of the enemy's greatest strategies against mothers is discouragement. Satan understands something powerful: if he can exhaust a praying mother emotionally, he can weaken spiritual perseverance.

Discouragement whispers:

"It will never change."

"Your prayers are useless."

"Nothing is happening."

"You have waited too long."

"Other people's children changed, but yours never will."

But discouragement lies. Because many miracles are already developing invisibly long before they become visible publicly.

Seeds underground appear lifeless before growth emerges.

Pregnancy itself reflects this principle. For months growth remains hidden before birth becomes visible.

The kingdom of God often works the same way.

God frequently moves invisibly before visibly.

This is why mothers must learn to trust what Heaven is doing beneath the surface.

The Syrophoenician woman in the New Testament reveals extraordinary perseverance.

Her daughter was grievously tormented, and she came desperately to Jesus for help. Yet what followed seems shocking.

At first, Jesus answered her not a word.

Silence.

Imagine how painful that moment must have felt.

This desperate mother approached the Savior carrying urgent need—and Heaven appeared silent.

Many mothers understand this feeling deeply.

Prayers seem unanswered.

Doors remain closed.

Breakthrough delays.

Yet the woman refused to walk away.

Even when others tried dismissing her, she continued pressing forward.

Eventually Jesus declared:

"O woman, great is thy faith..." — Matthew 15:28

Notice something profound:

Jesus did not merely honor her request. He honored her perseverance.

Sometimes persistence itself becomes proof of faith.

The woman's miracle was delayed, but not denied.

Many mothers abandon prayer too early because silence convinces them nothing is happening. But Heaven often works through process rather than instant intervention.

Elizabeth understood this deeply.

Luke 1 describes Elizabeth as righteous before God, yet barren. Years passed. Age advanced. Hope likely weakened gradually over time.

Imagine the private sorrow Elizabeth carried.

Imagine the prayers she prayed repeatedly.

Imagine the moments she wondered whether motherhood would ever happen.

Yet at the appointed time, God answered.

Not only did Elizabeth give birth—she gave birth to John the Baptist, a prophetic voice who would prepare the way for Christ Himself.

Sometimes delayed answers carry greater purpose than immediate ones.

This does not mean delay is easy.

Waiting can become emotionally exhausting.

Especially for mothers carrying long-term burdens.

A woman named Miriam understood this pain personally.

Her son Daniel became addicted to drugs during his teenage years. At first the family thought it was temporary rebellion. But the years became increasingly painful. Daniel stole money, lied repeatedly, disappeared for days, and eventually severed most family relationships.

Many people advised Miriam to give up emotionally.

Some even told her: *"Just move on with your life."*

But a mother's heart does not surrender easily. For eighteen years Miriam prayed.

Sometimes her prayers were filled with faith. Other times they were filled with tears.

There were nights she fell asleep exhausted after crying before God.

At times she became angry. At times confused. At times emotionally numb. Yet she continued praying.

One evening, after nearly two decades of addiction and brokenness, Daniel unexpectedly arrived at her home. He looked physically worn and emotionally shattered.

He simply said: *"Mom… I'm tired."*

That night became the beginning of restoration.

Recovery did not happen instantly. Healing unfolded through process. Relapses occurred. Counseling became necessary. Trust rebuilt slowly.

But prayer had kept a doorway open when destruction tried to close it permanently.

Years later Daniel became involved in helping young men overcome addiction.

Miriam eventually realized something profound:

God was not absent during the eighteen years.

He was working invisibly while she persevered visibly.

One of the deepest revelations about perseverance is this:

Sometimes God strengthens mothers through the very delay they wish to escape.

Waiting develops spiritual depth.

- ✓ *It exposes hidden fears.*
- ✓ *It reveals dependency upon outcomes rather than upon God Himself.*
- ✓ *It teaches surrender.*
- ✓ *It develops compassion.*
- ✓ *It deepens discernment.*
- ✓ *It builds endurance.*

And endurance produces spiritual stability.

Romans 5:3-4 says: *"Tribulation worketh patience; And patience, experience; and experience, hope."*

God often uses painful seasons to shape people into vessels capable of carrying greater spiritual weight.

This is why some mothers emerge from difficult seasons carrying unusual wisdom, compassion, authority, and discernment.

The storm that almost destroyed them eventually deepened them.

But perseverance requires intentional care because spiritual exhaustion is real.

Some mothers continue functioning outwardly while inwardly becoming depleted emotionally, spiritually, and mentally.

They pray mechanically.

Serve tirelessly.

Carry responsibilities endlessly.

Yet inside they feel numb.

Empty.

Tired.

Invisible.

Elijah experienced something similar after great spiritual victory. Despite witnessing God's power dramatically, emotional exhaustion overwhelmed him later.

This teaches an important truth:

Even strong people need restoration.
Mothers cannot pour endlessly without renewal.
This is why perseverance requires replenishment.
Praying mothers must also learn to rest spiritually.
Rest is not weakness. Jesus Himself withdrew regularly for prayer and renewal.
Mothers must stop believing they are required to carry everything alone constantly.
God never intended mothers to become emotional martyrs.
He invites them into partnership, not isolation.
Sometimes perseverance looks like continuing to pray.
Sometimes it looks like worshipping through tears.
Sometimes it looks like resting without quitting.
Sometimes it looks like choosing hope again after disappointment.
And sometimes perseverance simply means refusing to let bitterness replace faith.
One of the enemy's greatest goals during delay is to make mothers bitter instead of better.
Delayed answers can harden hearts if pain is not surrendered continually to God.
But surrendered pain becomes fertile ground for spiritual growth.
Tears offered to God never become wasted tears.
Psalm 56:8 says: *"Put thou my tears into thy bottle…"*
What a remarkable picture.
God notices tears. Heaven records sorrow. Pain matters to God.
No mother cries unnoticed before Him.
This chapter is especially important because many mothers today secretly carry silent disappointments. Some are waiting for prodigal children to return. Others are praying through infertility, emotional

estrangement, addiction, sickness, depression, or family breakdown.

And sometimes the greatest battle is not external—it is internal discouragement.

Yet perseverance is powerful because it keeps doors open for God's timing.

One prayer may not seem significant.

One year may not seem fruitful.

But persistent faith builds spiritual momentum over time.

And often, just before breakthrough comes, exhaustion intensifies.

This is why Galatians 6:9 remains so powerful:

"In due season we shall reap, if we faint not."

Due season exists.

Even if unseen presently.

Even if delayed presently.

Even if misunderstood presently.

God's timing is never careless.

And sometimes what feels like silence is actually preparation.

Preparation within children.

Preparation within circumstances.

Preparation within mothers themselves.

One day many mothers will look back and realize:

God was working the entire time.

Even during silence.

Even during delay.

Even during tears.

And perhaps the deepest revelation in this chapter is this:

Perseverance is love refusing to surrender hope.

A praying mother continues believing when visible evidence disappears.

She continues planting while waiting.

Continues trusting while hurting.
Continues interceding while exhausted.
And Heaven honors that perseverance deeply.

Handling Discouragement

Discouragement grows when mothers focus only on visible circumstances.
Faith grows when mothers remember God's character.
Learn to:

- ✓ *Return continually to Scripture*
- ✓ *Pray honestly, not performatively*
- ✓ *Surround yourself with faith-filled relationships*
- ✓ *Celebrate small signs of progress*
- ✓ *Remember previous faithfulness from God*

Fighting Spiritual Exhaustion

Exhaustion weakens discernment and hope.
Mothers need:

- ✓ *Spiritual rest*
- ✓ *Quiet time with God*
- ✓ *Healthy emotional support*
- ✓ *Moments of renewal*
- ✓ *Permission to grieve honestly*

Even Jesus rested.

Maintaining Faith Through Delay

Faith through delay requires:

- ✓ *Trusting God's timing*
- ✓ *Refusing bitterness*
- ✓ *Continuing spiritual disciplines*
- ✓ *Speaking life despite circumstances*
- ✓ *Believing God still works invisibly*

Delay is not abandonment.

Reflection Questions

- ✓ *What delayed prayer has challenged my faith most deeply?*
- ✓ *Have I confused God's silence with God's absence?*
- ✓ *What discouragements repeatedly attack my thoughts?*
- ✓ *Am I emotionally exhausted spiritually?*
- ✓ *How has waiting changed me personally?*

Practical Action Plan

Step 1: Strengthen Spiritual Consistency

Continue praying, worshipping, and reading Scripture even when emotions fluctuate.

Step 2: Guard Against Bitterness

Release disappointment honestly before God rather than allowing hidden resentment to grow.

Step 3: Record Signs of Hope

Keep a journal documenting answered prayers, small breakthroughs, encouraging words, and moments of growth.

Family Exercise

As a family, share one prayer request each person is still waiting on. Pray together intentionally and encourage one another through Scripture.

Declaration

"My prayers are not wasted. Heaven hears every cry, records every tear, and works beyond what I can presently see. I will not surrender to discouragement. In due season, God's promises will unfold."

Prayer for Perseverance

Heavenly Father,

Strengthen me in seasons when Heaven seems silent. When I grow weary emotionally, renew my spirit. When discouragement whispers lies, remind me that You are still working invisibly.

Help me persevere without becoming bitter. Teach me to trust Your timing even when I do not understand the process. Heal disappointment within my heart and restore hope where exhaustion has weakened faith.

I surrender every prodigal child, every delayed answer, every painful burden, and every unanswered question into Your hands. Let my tears become seeds before You. And help me continue believing until breakthrough comes.

In Jesus' name, Amen.

CHAPTER 6
PAIN
"The Tears God Stores"

"Thou tellest my wanderings: put thou my tears into thy bottle: are they not in thy book?"
— Psalm 56:8

There are tears that nobody sees.
Tears hidden behind bathroom doors.
Tears released silently after children fall asleep.
Tears buried beneath smiles at church.
Tears mothers wipe away quickly because life does not pause for grief.
Some tears come from disappointment.
Others from betrayal.
Others from exhaustion.
Others from loneliness.
Others from watching children suffer while feeling powerless to stop the pain.
And one of the deepest struggles mothers face is this: many continue carrying responsibilities while silently bleeding internally.
Yet Scripture reveals something astonishing:
God stores tears.
Heaven notices pain.
No tear surrendered to God is ever wasted.
This is one of the most healing revelations a wounded mother can receive. Human beings often overlook pain they cannot see. Society celebrates strength but rarely understands hidden sorrow. Many mothers become experts at functioning outwardly while quietly collapsing inwardly.
But God sees differently.

Psalm 56:8 paints one of the most intimate pictures in Scripture: *"Put thou my tears into thy bottle…"*
Imagine that image carefully.
The Creator of the universe values human tears enough to preserve them.
What people dismiss casually, Heaven records carefully.
What others forget, God remembers.
What wounds silently, God notices deeply.
This means pain is not meaningless when surrendered to God.
Pain offered honestly before God becomes intercession.
One of the greatest misunderstandings about spiritual strength is the assumption that strong people do not break emotionally. Yet throughout Scripture, some of the strongest people walked through profound sorrow.
Brokenness itself is not weakness.
Unprocessed pain is dangerous.
But surrendered pain becomes sacred ground where God often develops spiritual depth.
Some mothers reading this chapter carry wounds nobody around them fully understands.

- ✓ *Some were abandoned emotionally.*
- ✓ *Some survived betrayal.*
- ✓ *Some buried dreams.*
- ✓ *Some lost loved ones.*
- ✓ *Some carry trauma from childhood itself.*
- ✓ *Some feel exhausted from years of carrying families through crisis after crisis.*

And quietly many wonder:
"How do I continue loving, nurturing, praying, and building others while hurting myself?"
The answer begins here:

God heals what mothers surrender honestly.
Psalm 147:3 declares: "He healeth the broken in heart, and bindeth up their wounds."
Notice that God does not merely acknowledge wounds.
He heals them.
This is deeply important because many mothers attempt to function spiritually while ignoring emotional pain internally. They continue serving others while secretly becoming emotionally numb, angry, fearful, or exhausted.
But buried pain does not disappear.
Ignored wounds often leak into parenting.
Hurt people unintentionally hurt others.
Fear becomes control.
Rejection becomes harshness.
Betrayal becomes distrust.
Unhealed shame becomes constant criticism.
Emotional exhaustion becomes irritability.
This is why healing matters spiritually.
God does not merely want mothers productive.
He wants them whole.
One of the enemy's greatest strategies is convincing wounded mothers that their pain disqualifies them from purpose. But throughout Scripture, God repeatedly works through broken people.
In fact, broken mothers often raise spiritually strong children.
Why? Because suffering frequently develops depth that comfort never produces.
Pain teaches dependence upon God differently.
Brokenness deepens compassion.
Sorrow develops sensitivity.
And tears often become the birthplace of spiritual authority.

Hagar understood this kind of pain.
Her story is filled with rejection, loneliness, fear, and survival. Cast away into the wilderness with her son Ishmael, Hagar found herself emotionally overwhelmed and physically desperate.
Genesis 21 reveals one of the most heartbreaking moments in Scripture. Unable to bear watching her child suffer, Hagar placed Ishmael under a shrub and withdrew, weeping in anguish.
Many mothers understand this feeling.
The helplessness of watching children suffer.
The ache of carrying burdens too heavy emotionally.
The fear of not knowing how situations will end.
Yet in the wilderness, God revealed Himself to Hagar personally.
Scripture says: *"And God heard the voice of the lad…"* — Genesis 21:17
The God who sees met the mother who was breaking.
And perhaps that is one of the greatest revelations within pain:
God often reveals Himself most intimately in wilderness seasons.
Many people know God intellectually.
But wounded mothers often know Him personally.
Not as distant theology, but as sustainer.
Provider.
Comforter.
Healer.
Protector.
This same truth appears powerfully in Mary, the mother of Jesus.
Most people celebrate Mary at the manger.
But fewer speak about Mary at the cross.

The same mother who once held Jesus as a child eventually stood watching Him crucified publicly.
Imagine the agony.
The helplessness.
The grief.
Simeon had prophesied years earlier:
"Yea, a sword shall pierce through thy own soul also…" — Luke 2:35
Mary's pain was not accidental.
It became part of her spiritual journey.
One of the painful truths mothers eventually learn is that loving deeply also creates vulnerability to grief deeply.
The deeper the love, the deeper the ache when children suffer.
Yet Mary remained present.
Even at the cross.
Pain did not remove her love.
And sometimes the greatest ministry mothers offer is faithful presence during painful seasons.
Not all pain can be fixed immediately.
But love remains.
Naomi's story reveals another dimension of pain.
By the opening chapter of Ruth, Naomi had lost her husband and both sons. Her grief became so overwhelming that she declared:
"Call me not Naomi, call me Mara: for the Almighty hath dealt very bitterly with me." — Ruth 1:20
Pain changed how Naomi saw herself.
That happens often in suffering.
Unhealed pain distorts identity.
Disappointment can convince mothers they are forgotten, abandoned, or empty.
But Naomi's story did not end in bitterness.

God eventually restored purpose through Ruth and future generations connected to her lineage.
This is important because many mothers mistakenly assume painful seasons permanently define their future.
But God specializes in redemption.
He restores what grief attempted to destroy.
He rebuilds what sorrow weakened.
He heals what trauma fractured.
And He often produces beauty from ashes gradually.
One of the deepest revelations in this chapter is this:
Pain surrendered to God becomes spiritual strength instead of hidden poison.
Some mothers suppress pain instead of healing from it.
They continue functioning outwardly while inwardly carrying resentment, fear, shame, disappointment, or emotional exhaustion.
But hidden wounds eventually affect atmosphere within homes.
Children absorb emotional climates deeply.
A mother constantly operating from unresolved fear may unintentionally raise anxious children.
A mother carrying bitterness may unknowingly create emotional distance.
A mother overwhelmed internally may struggle to nurture consistently.
This is why healing is not selfish.
Healing protects generations.
One of the enemy's greatest goals is generational transmission of unresolved pain.
Wounded parents often reproduce wounded environments unintentionally.
But a praying mother can reverse generational destruction.

Healing can begin with one surrendered life.
A woman named Grace experienced this powerfully.
After her husband died unexpectedly in an accident, Grace suddenly found herself raising three children alone. Financial pressure mounted quickly. Fear overwhelmed her constantly. At night, after her children slept, she often cried privately wondering how she would survive emotionally and practically.
Her youngest daughter, Lily, began struggling emotionally after the loss. She became withdrawn and fearful, constantly asking whether other loved ones would disappear too.
Grace realized something important:
If she allowed grief to consume her completely, her children would inherit fear instead of healing.
This did not mean pretending pain did not exist.
Instead, Grace began surrendering pain honestly to God.
She prayed openly with her children.
They cried together sometimes.
They spoke honestly about loss.
But Grace also intentionally created moments of hope within the home.
Worship music filled difficult evenings.
Scripture became comfort.
Prayer became survival.
Years later Lily shared something remarkable with her mother:
"Mom, watching you trust God while hurting taught me that pain doesn't have to destroy us."
Grace eventually realized her greatest testimony was not avoiding pain—but surviving it with faith intact.
Broken mothers often become powerful healers because they understand suffering personally.

2 Corinthians 1:4 says God comforts us so we may comfort others.

Pain can either harden hearts or deepen compassion.

The difference depends upon surrender.

This is why forgiveness becomes critically important in healing.

Many mothers carry hidden resentment toward people who wounded them deeply—former spouses, absent fathers, abusive parents, betraying friends, or even children themselves.

And unresolved bitterness quietly poisons emotional health.

Forgiveness does not excuse wrong behavior.

It releases the wounded heart from becoming chained permanently to pain.

Jesus Himself modeled forgiveness even during suffering.

"Father, forgive them…" — Luke 23:34

Forgiveness is often less about feelings and more about surrendering judgment into God's hands.

Many mothers wait until emotions change before forgiving.

But healing frequently begins with obedience before feelings fully align.

This process may take time.

Deep wounds rarely heal instantly.

God often heals layer by layer.

Moment by moment.

Prayer by prayer.

And one of the most beautiful truths mothers must remember is this:

God is patient with healing.

Some women reading this chapter feel emotionally exhausted because they have carried pain silently for years. Perhaps they fear appearing weak. Perhaps others depend heavily upon them. Perhaps survival mode became normal.

But healing begins when mothers stop pretending they are unbreakable.

Jesus never rejected broken people.

He moved toward them.

The woman with the issue of blood.

Blind Bartimaeus.

The grieving widow.

Mary Magdalene.

The brokenhearted were drawn toward Christ because He carried healing presence.

And He still does.

One of the greatest gifts mothers can give their children is not perfection.

It is healed wholeness.

Children do not need flawless mothers. They need authentic mothers who allow God to heal them continually.

- ✓ *Mothers who apologize when wrong.*
- ✓ *Mothers who process pain healthily.*
- ✓ *Mothers who forgive sincerely.*
- ✓ *Mothers who demonstrate resilience through faith.*

Mothers who teach that tears are not weakness.

Because tears surrendered to God become seeds.

- ✓ *Seeds of healing.*
- ✓ *Seeds of wisdom.*
- ✓ *Seeds of compassion.*
- ✓ *Seeds of spiritual authority.*

And sometimes the mothers who cried the deepest eventually become the strongest pillars within future generations.

Not because suffering was easy.

But because God met them faithfully within it.

Healing Inner Wounds

Healing begins with honesty before God.

Mothers must stop minimizing emotional pain and begin surrendering it prayerfully.

God heals:

Rejection

Betrayal

Grief

Shame

Fear

Emotional exhaustion

Trauma from past experiences

Healing is a journey, not a performance.

Learning Forgiveness

Forgiveness frees the heart from permanent bondage to pain.

It does not deny hurt. It releases bitterness.

Forgiveness allows healing to begin where resentment once ruled.

Restoring Emotional Strength

Emotional restoration requires:

- ✓ *Time with God*
- ✓ *Honest prayer*
- ✓ *Supportive relationships*
- ✓ *Rest*
- ✓ *Healthy boundaries*
- ✓ *Speaking truth instead of fear*

Even strong mothers need replenishment.

Reflection Questions

- ✓ *What pain have I been carrying silently?*

- ✓ *Have unresolved wounds affected my parenting?*
- ✓ *What fears or bitterness need surrender to God?*
- ✓ *Do my children experience peace or emotional heaviness from me?*
- ✓ *What areas of my heart still need healing?*

Practical Action Plan

Step 1: Bring Pain Into God's Presence

Spend intentional time praying honestly about hidden wounds and disappointments.

Step 2: Begin the Process of Forgiveness

Write down names, situations, or memories requiring surrender and healing.

Step 3: Build Emotional Restoration Rhythms

Create space for prayer, rest, worship, healthy conversations, and emotional renewal regularly.

Family Exercise

Create a family gratitude and healing evening. Allow each family member to share one difficult experience and one thing God has helped them overcome.

Declaration

"My pain will not destroy future generations. God is healing my heart, restoring my strength, and transforming my tears into seeds of wisdom, compassion, and spiritual authority."

Prayer for Healing

Heavenly Father,

You see every hidden tear and every wound buried deep within my heart. Nothing about my pain is invisible to You. Thank You for being near to the brokenhearted.

Heal the places within me still carrying fear, grief, rejection, bitterness, disappointment, and exhaustion. Teach me how to surrender pain instead of hiding it. Restore emotional strength where life has weakened me.

Help me forgive those who wounded me deeply. Remove every root of bitterness and replace it with peace. Let healing flow not only through my life but through future generations connected to me.

And Lord, transform my tears into seeds that produce wisdom, compassion, resilience, and faith within my children and family.

In Jesus'name, Amen.

CHAPTER 7
PROPHECY
"Speaking Life Over Generations"

"Death and life are in the power of the tongue..."
— Proverbs 18:21

Words are never empty.
They carry weight.
They shape atmosphere.
They build identity.
They wound hearts or heal them.
They can imprison a child emotionally for years—or release courage, confidence, healing, and destiny.
One of the greatest unseen powers God has placed within a mother is the power of her words.
A mother may forget certain sentences she spoke casually, but children often remember them for decades.
Some adults still hear the echo of words spoken over them in childhood.
"You'll never succeed."
"You always fail."
"Why can't you be like others?"
"You are difficult."
"You are unwanted."
Negative words become internal strongholds when repeated consistently.
But the opposite is also true.
Words filled with life become prophetic seeds.
"I believe in you."
"God has a purpose for your life."
"You are loved."
"You are not defined by failure."

"You will overcome."
"You are stronger than this season."
Children often become what they repeatedly hear spoken over them.
This is why mothers must understand that their words help create spiritual atmosphere within the home.
Atmosphere is invisible, yet deeply powerful.
Some homes feel heavy constantly. Others feel peaceful.
Some feel filled with fear. Others feel filled with hope.
And words play a major role in shaping that environment.
Ephesians 4:29 says: *"Let no corrupt communication proceed out of your mouth, but that which is good to the use of edifying..."*
The word *"edifying"* means building up.
Words either build or break.
Strengthen or weaken.
Heal or wound.
This does not mean mothers must pretend problems do not exist. Biblical encouragement is not denial. Speaking life does not ignore reality—it speaks God's perspective into reality.
This is deeply important because many mothers unknowingly speak frustration more consistently than faith.
Correction becomes constant.
Criticism becomes habitual.
Fear-filled predictions dominate conversations.
And over time, children internalize these atmospheres.
A child repeatedly called "useless" may eventually stop trying.

A child constantly compared may develop deep insecurity.

A child raised around hopeless speech may eventually believe nothing good awaits them.

Words become internal architecture.

They shape how children view themselves, others, and even God.

This is why prophetic mothers speak life intentionally.

Not manipulation.

Not fantasy.

But truth aligned with God's heart.

Ezekiel 37 reveals one of the most powerful pictures of prophetic speech in Scripture.

God brought Ezekiel into a valley filled with dry bones and asked: *"Can these bones live?"*

Naturally speaking, the situation looked impossible.

Dead.

Hopeless.

Irrecoverable.

Yet God instructed Ezekiel to prophesy.

To speak life where death appeared dominant.

And as he spoke, movement began.

Bones connected.

Breath entered.

Life emerged.

This passage reveals something profound:

God often partners with spoken words to release transformation.

Many mothers today are standing emotionally inside valleys of dry bones.

Children seem spiritually cold.

Relationships appear fractured.

Hope feels exhausted.

Situations look beyond repair.

Yet Heaven still asks: *"Can these bones live?"*

And prophetic mothers learn to speak life even before visible change appears.

Not because circumstances look perfect. But because God still works resurrection.

One of the greatest battles mothers face is resisting the temptation to speak only according to current circumstances.

When children struggle repeatedly, negative speech becomes easy.

"This child will never change."

"He always disappoints us."

"She cannot handle responsibility."

"He is just rebellious."

But labels become dangerous when repeated continually.

Children often rise or fall toward the identities spoken over them consistently.

This is why prophetic speech matters deeply.

Prophetic speech is not merely emotional positivity.

It is speaking according to God's potential rather than temporary failure.

Jesus Himself modeled this repeatedly.

Simon was unstable, impulsive, and inconsistent. Yet Jesus called him Peter—a rock.

Gideon felt fearful, yet God called him *"mighty man of valor."*

Abram became Abraham before nations emerged.

God frequently speaks destiny before manifestation.

Prophetic mothers learn to do the same.

Mary understood this power deeply.

Luke 1 records Mary's extraordinary prophetic song after receiving God's promise concerning Jesus. *"My soul doth magnify the Lord…"* — Luke 1:46

Mary spoke faith before fulfillment. She worshipped before manifestation. She declared God's greatness while still carrying unseen promise.
This is important because many mothers wait for circumstances to improve before speaking hope.
But prophetic mothers speak life during process.
Not after victory alone. During process.
Mary's words created atmosphere for what Heaven was birthing.
And mothers still carry this spiritual influence today.
Elizabeth also demonstrated prophetic speech powerfully.
When Mary visited her, Elizabeth immediately began speaking blessing, affirmation, and confirmation: *"Blessed art thou among women…"* — Luke 1:42
Notice the atmosphere Elizabeth created. She strengthened rather than discouraged.
Affirmed rather than criticized. Confirmed rather than questioned.
Some people drain faith from others. Prophetic people strengthen it.
Mothers must recognize that children desperately need voices of life within a world filled with criticism, comparison, confusion, and insecurity.
Modern culture constantly attacks identity.
Children today grow up surrounded by pressure to perform, compete, compare, and prove worth externally.
Social media intensifies insecurity daily.
Many children secretly battle feelings of inadequacy.
This is why a mother's words matter more than ever before.
Children need homes where identity is reinforced spiritually, not merely performance-driven.

One of the greatest tragedies is when children feel safer receiving affirmation from strangers than from family.
A mother's voice should become a place of life.
Not perfection.
But life.
This becomes especially important during seasons when children fail.
Failure often reveals the atmosphere within homes.
Some homes respond with shame.
Others respond with wisdom and restoration.
Jesus modeled restorative speech beautifully with Peter after Peter denied Him three times. Jesus corrected Peter, yet He never discarded Peter's destiny. Failure did not become Peter's permanent identity.
Wise mothers understand this balance.
Correction matters.
Accountability matters.
But identity must remain anchored beyond temporary mistakes.

A woman named Rebecca learned this deeply with her son Aaron.
Aaron struggled academically throughout school. Teachers repeatedly labeled him lazy, distracted, and incapable. Relatives constantly compared him with other children who performed better academically.
Over time Aaron began believing he was a failure.
His confidence deteriorated slowly.
He stopped trying. Stopped participating. Stopped believing in himself.
But Rebecca sensed something others overlooked.

Though Aaron struggled academically, he possessed unusual creativity and compassion. He loved repairing broken things, helping neighbors, and working with his hands.
Instead of repeating negative labels, Rebecca intentionally began speaking differently over him.
"Aaron, God created you with purpose."
"You are not less valuable because you learn differently."
"You have wisdom and creativity inside you."
"You are not a failure."
At first Aaron resisted her encouragement because years of criticism had shaped his identity deeply.
But Rebecca continued consistently.
She prayed over him nightly.
Spoke blessing regularly.
Encouraged his strengths intentionally.
Years later Aaron became highly skilled in engineering design and mentoring struggling teenagers.
One evening he told his mother: *"Mom, your words kept me alive emotionally when I had stopped believing in myself."*
Words matter. Especially repeated words.
Some mothers underestimate the spiritual authority carried within daily speech.
But homes are built verbally long before they are built emotionally.
Fear-filled words create fearful atmospheres.
Angry words create tense environments.
Hopeless words create emotional heaviness.
But life-giving words create courage.
Peace.
Identity.
Security.

Expectation.
This does not mean mothers should become fake or superficial. Authenticity matters deeply. Children recognize dishonesty quickly.
But prophetic speech means choosing words aligned with truth rather than hopelessness.
Instead of:
"You always fail."
Say:
"You made a mistake, but mistakes do not define who you are."
Instead of:
"You will never change."
Say:
"I believe God is still working in your life."
Instead of:
"Our family is ruined."
Say:
"This season is painful, but God restores broken things."
Prophetic mothers become guardians of atmosphere. They understand that repeated words eventually become internal beliefs.
One of the most practical ways mothers can cultivate prophetic atmosphere is through intentional blessing.
Throughout Scripture, blessings carried spiritual significance.
Isaac blessing Jacob.
Jacob blessing his sons.
Jesus blessing children.
Blessing is more than emotional encouragement—it is intentional life-giving speech released through faith.
Many children today rarely hear spoken blessing consistently.

They hear instructions.
Corrections.
Warnings.
But little blessing.
Yet blessing nourishes identity.
Some children grow emotionally thirsty for affirmation because criticism became louder than encouragement.
This is why intentional blessing prayers matter.
Simple spoken words can shape hearts profoundly.
"God has good plans for your future."
"You are deeply loved."
"I thank God for your life."
"You carry strength and purpose."
"The Lord will guide and protect you."
These moments may appear small, but repeated blessing builds emotional and spiritual stability over time.
Another powerful tool is identity statements rooted in Scripture.
Children must learn identity from God before culture defines them incorrectly.
Teach children:
"You are fearfully and wonderfully made."
"You are chosen."
"You are loved by God."
"You are never alone."
"You were created with purpose."
Identity anchored spiritually becomes protection against cultural confusion.
This matters because many young people today suffer identity crises not because they lack talent, but because they lack rootedness.
And mothers help establish that rootedness.
One of the deepest revelations in this chapter is this:

Children often borrow belief from their mothers before developing belief within themselves.

Before children fully understand destiny, mothers often carry vision for them first.

This is why words spoken repeatedly become prophetic architecture.

Not every child responds immediately.

Some children resist.

Some wander temporarily.

Some battle insecurity deeply.

But seeds planted verbally over years continue working internally.

A mother's words often outlive her presence.

Long after conversations end, sentences remain alive inside hearts.

Many adults still draw strength from words spoken by praying mothers decades earlier.

And sadly, many still battle wounds from destructive words too.

This is why mothers must become careful stewards of speech.

Not perfect.

But intentional.

Because prophetic mothers do more than raise children.

They shape generations through atmosphere, identity, and life-giving words.

And sometimes the miracle begins not when circumstances change externally—

But when words change internally within the home.

Speaking Daily Declarations

Daily declarations help establish spiritual atmosphere.

Speak intentionally:

- ✓ *God's protection*
- ✓ *God's purpose*
- ✓ *God's wisdom*
- ✓ *God's peace*
- ✓ *God's favor*
- ✓ *God's strength*

Repeated truth builds inner stability.

Blessing Prayers Over Children

Pray blessings aloud regularly:

- ✓ *Before school*
- ✓ *Before sleep*
- ✓ *During difficult seasons*
- ✓ *Before important decisions*
- ✓ *During emotional struggles*

Children flourish when consistently covered with life-giving words.

Building Identity Statements

Teach children identity through Scripture rather than culture.

Examples:

"I am loved by God."
"God has purpose for my life."
"I can overcome through Christ."
"I am never abandoned."

Identity protects destiny.

Reflection Questions

- ✓ *What atmosphere do my words create within my home?*
- ✓ *What phrases do my children hear repeatedly from me?*
- ✓ *Have frustration and criticism become stronger than encouragement?*

- ✓ *What labels have I unknowingly spoken over my children?*
- ✓ *How can I intentionally build identity through words?*

Practical Action Plan

Step 1: Evaluate Speech Patterns

Pay attention to recurring words, tones, and labels used within the home.

Step 2: Begin Speaking Intentional Blessing

Speak encouragement, hope, and truth consistently over children daily.

Step 3: Create Scripture-Based Identity Habits

Choose biblical declarations to pray and repeat regularly as a family.

Family Exercise

Have each family member speak one encouraging statement and one blessing over every other family member aloud.

Declaration

"My words will build, not break. I will create an atmosphere of life, truth, hope, healing, and identity within my home. My children will grow rooted in God's purpose and not in fear, shame, or insecurity."

Prayer for Prophetic Speech

Heavenly Father,

Teach me to use my words wisely and life-givingly. Forgive me for every careless, fearful, angry, or destructive word I have spoken. Help me create an atmosphere within my home that reflects Your heart.

Teach me to speak life over my children even during difficult seasons. Let my words strengthen identity, restore hope, and build faith. Remove every negative label, every curse of comparison, and every atmosphere of discouragement from our family.

Help my children know who they are through Your truth and not through the confusion of this world. Let blessing, peace, wisdom, and purpose flow through our conversations daily.

And may my words become seeds that strengthen generations long after I am gone.

In Jesus' name, Amen.

PART 2
THE BATTLES OF A PRAYING MOTHER

CHAPTER 8
THE BATTLE OF FEAR

"Fear thou not; for I am with thee…"
— Isaiah 41:10

For God hath not given us the spirit of fear; but of power, and of love, and of a sound mind." — 2 Timothy 1:7

Few battles torment a mother's heart more deeply than fear.

Fear often hides behind love.

The deeper the love, the greater the temptation to fear losing, failing, hurting, or watching children suffer.

A mother may smile publicly while privately carrying terrifying thoughts.

"What if something happens to my child?"
"What if I fail as a parent?"
"What if my children choose the wrong path?"
"What if I cannot protect them?"
"What if the world changes them?"

Fear is one of the enemy's oldest weapons against mothers because fear distorts perspective, weakens peace, clouds discernment, and slowly shifts trust away from God toward anxiety.

And modern parenting has intensified this battle dramatically.

Today's mothers carry fears previous generations rarely faced in the same way.

- ✓ *Fear of digital influence.*
- ✓ *Fear of addiction.*
- ✓ *Fear of depression.*
- ✓ *Fear of moral confusion.*
- ✓ *Fear of violence.*

- ✓ *Fear of peer pressure.*
- ✓ *Fear of failure.*
- ✓ *Fear of losing connection with children emotionally.*
- ✓ *Fear of not doing enough.*
- ✓ *Fear of future uncertainty.*

Many mothers today are emotionally exhausted not because they do not love deeply—but because they fear constantly.

And fear is draining.

Fear causes mothers to overthink constantly.

Overprotect constantly.

Worry constantly.

Imagine worst-case scenarios constantly.

Even when nothing is presently wrong.

Fear quietly steals peace before problems even arrive.

This is why Scripture repeatedly commands: *"Fear not."*

Not because dangers never exist. But because fear itself becomes spiritually destructive when it controls the heart.

Fear is not merely an emotion.

Uncontrolled fear becomes an atmosphere.

And atmospheres shape homes.

Children raised inside constant fear often absorb anxiety silently.

A fearful home may become emotionally tense, overly controlling, suspicious, or unstable without realizing it.

Children can sense fear even when words are not spoken openly.

This is why mothers must learn the difference between wisdom and fear.

Wisdom prepares.

Fear panics.
Wisdom discerns.
Fear imagines catastrophe continually.
Wisdom trusts God while acting responsibly.
Fear attempts to control everything because it struggles to trust.
One of the deepest revelations mothers must understand is this:
Fear grows wherever trust weakens.
The battle of fear is ultimately a battle over trust.
Will mothers trust circumstances more than God?
Will they trust news headlines more than God's promises?
Will they trust visible problems more than Heaven's ability to intervene?
Isaiah 41:10 speaks directly into fearful hearts: *"Fear thou not; for I am with thee: be not dismayed; for I am thy God…"*
Notice that God does not merely say: *"Do not fear."*
He explains why.
"For I am with thee."
The antidote to fear is not perfect circumstances.
It is God's presence.
Many mothers are waiting for life to become predictable before experiencing peace. But biblical peace does not come from controlling outcomes. It comes from confidence that God remains present even within uncertainty.
Jochebed, the mother of Moses, understood this battle deeply.
Imagine the terror surrounding Moses' birth. Pharaoh had ordered Hebrew male children to be killed. Every mother in Israel lived under unimaginable fear.
Yet Hebrews 11:23 says something remarkable: *"By faith Moses… was hid three months of his parents…"*

Notice the phrase: *"By faith."*
Not by fear.
Jochebed certainly felt fear emotionally. Any mother would. But fear did not become her master. She acted through faith. She hid Moses. Prepared strategically. Trusted God courageously. And eventually released him into God's hands upon the Nile River.
That moment reveals one of the hardest lessons mothers ever learn:
Children ultimately belong to God.
Mothers steward children lovingly, but they cannot control every outcome, every decision, or every future moment.
And fear intensifies whenever mothers attempt to carry responsibilities only God can carry fully.
Many mothers secretly live burdened by impossible pressure.

- ✓ *Pressure to protect children from every pain.*
- ✓ *Pressure to guarantee successful outcomes.*
- ✓ *Pressure to prevent every mistake.*
- ✓ *Pressure to control every influence.*

But no mother was designed to function as God.
This realization is not weakness. It is freedom.
Prayer becomes powerful because it reaches where parenting cannot.
There are places a mother's hands cannot reach. But prayer can.
A mother cannot always stand beside her child physically at school, at work, in relationships, during temptations, or during moments of crisis. But God can.
Fear often grows strongest where mothers feel powerless.
This is why prayer matters so deeply.

Prayer transfers burdens from limited human control into God's sovereign hands.

One of the greatest struggles in modern parenting is fear about the future.

"What kind of world will my children inherit?"

"Will they remain spiritually strong?"

"Will culture destroy their convictions?"

Many mothers today feel overwhelmed by how rapidly society changes. Moral confusion increases. Digital influence dominates. Family structures weaken. Emotional instability rises.

And many mothers secretly wonder: *"How do I raise godly children in a world like this?"*

But Scripture reminds us that God has always raised strong people in difficult times.

Moses was raised during oppression.

Daniel was raised in Babylon.

Esther lived within a pagan empire.

Timothy grew spiritually within a corrupt Roman culture.

God is not intimidated by difficult generations.

In fact, He often raises the strongest voices during the darkest seasons.

This is why mothers must stop parenting primarily through fear and begin parenting through faith-filled intentionality.

Fear produces panic. Faith produces wisdom.

Fear creates emotional instability. Faith creates spiritual steadiness.

One of the enemy's goals is making mothers so anxious about the future that they become emotionally unavailable in the present.

Fear steals today while worrying about tomorrow.

Jesus addressed this directly in Matthew 6: *"Take therefore no thought for the morrow…"*

Jesus was not promoting irresponsibility. He was confronting anxious living.

Fear-filled parenting often becomes overly controlling parenting.

Some mothers attempt to manage every detail of children's lives because fear convinces them disaster will happen otherwise.

But excessive control can unintentionally damage trust and emotional connection.

Fear often disguises itself as protection.

Yet children also need space to grow, mature, make decisions, learn responsibility, and develop personal relationship with God themselves.

Mothers cannot permanently replace the Holy Spirit in their children's lives.

Eventually children must learn to hear God personally.

This is why wise mothers prepare children spiritually instead of controlling them endlessly.

Preparation builds maturity. Fear builds dependency.

A woman named Lydia experienced this battle intensely.

After hearing repeated stories about violence, addiction, and peer pressure affecting teenagers, Lydia became consumed with fear concerning her son Nathan. She monitored everything obsessively. Every delayed phone call created panic. Every new friendship produced suspicion.

Slowly Nathan became emotionally distant.

Not because Lydia lacked love.

But because fear had begun controlling the atmosphere within the home.

One evening Nathan finally said: *"Mom, it feels like you believe something bad will always happen to me."*

That sentence pierced Lydia deeply.

She realized fear had slowly become louder than faith.

That night she prayed honestly before God, confessing her anxiety and surrendering her son again into God's hands.

The situation did not change overnight.

But Lydia slowly learned to parent from peace rather than panic.

She continued guiding wisely. Continued setting boundaries. Continued praying intentionally. But she stopped allowing fear to dominate every conversation and decision. Over time Nathan became more open emotionally because trust replaced tension.

One of the greatest revelations mothers must understand is this: Fear and faith both imagine the future differently.

Fear imagines disaster.

Faith imagines God's presence within every future season.

This does not mean faith ignores danger or difficulty.

Faith simply refuses to believe evil will have final authority.

2 Timothy 1:7 declares: *"For God hath not given us the spirit of fear…"*

Notice that fear is described spiritually. Fear is not always harmless emotion.

Persistent fear can become spiritual oppression.

It weakens clarity.

Destroys peace.

Creates torment.

And gradually drains emotional strength.

But the verse continues: *"…but of power, and of love, and of a sound mind."*

God gives power instead of helplessness. Love instead of panic.
A sound mind instead of tormenting thoughts.
Many mothers today need restoration of soundness within their minds. Endless exposure to frightening news, comparisons, social pressures, and worst-case thinking has left many emotionally overwhelmed. But God desires mothers to live anchored, not tormented.
Peaceful, not paralyzed.
Watchful, but not fearful.
One of the enemy's greatest strategies is convincing mothers that fear equals responsibility.
But fear is not wisdom.
Constant anxiety does not protect children spiritually. Prayer does. Discernment does. Intentional parenting does. Healthy communication does. Spiritual atmosphere does.
Fear itself saves nobody.
This becomes especially important because children often inherit emotional patterns from environments around them.
Fearful homes often produce fearful children.
Anxious parents unintentionally raise anxious atmospheres.
But peaceful mothers create emotional safety.
This does not mean mothers never struggle emotionally.
It means they continually return fear to God instead of allowing fear to rule internally.
David demonstrated this beautifully in Psalm 56:3: *"What time I am afraid, I will trust in thee."*
Notice David did not deny fear existed. He redirected it. Fear itself may arise emotionally. But mothers must choose where fear leads them.

Toward panic? Or toward prayer?
Toward control? Or toward trust?
Toward despair? Or toward God's promises?

One of the deepest acts of spiritual maturity is learning how to surrender children repeatedly into God's hands.

Not once. Repeatedly.

Because every new season introduces fresh opportunities for fear.

School years.
Teenage years.
Friendships.
Marriage decisions.
Health concerns.
Career paths.
Adulthood.

Mothers never completely stop caring deeply.

But mature mothers learn to release fear continually instead of allowing it to dominate their hearts.

And perhaps this is one of the deepest revelations in this chapter:

Fear shrinks vision, but faith expands perspective.

Fear focuses constantly on what may go wrong.

Faith remembers Who remains sovereign even when life feels uncertain.

A praying mother may still feel concern. Still feel burdened. Still cry. Still wrestle emotionally. But she refuses to let fear become the loudest voice within her life.

Because she knows something powerful:

The same God who entrusted those children to her is able to sustain, guide, protect, restore, and pursue them far beyond her own human ability.

And when mothers finally surrender fear fully into God's hands, peace slowly returns to the home.

Not because life becomes perfect. But because trust becomes stronger than terror.

Reflection Questions

- ✓ *What fears dominate my thoughts most often concerning my children?*
- ✓ *Have I confused fear with wisdom?*
- ✓ *How has fear affected the atmosphere within my home?*
- ✓ *Am I parenting through peace or through anxiety?*
- ✓ *What burdens do I need to surrender back to God?*

Practical Action Plan

Step 1: Identify Fear Triggers

Recognize situations, thoughts, or influences that repeatedly create anxiety and bring them prayerfully before God.

Step 2: Replace Fear With Scripture

Speak God's promises aloud whenever fearful thoughts arise.

Step 3: Practice Daily Surrender

Intentionally place your children, their future, and your concerns into God's hands through prayer each day.

Family Exercise

As a family, discuss one fear each person carries. Pray together specifically over those fears and read Isaiah 41:10 aloud together.

Declaration

"I will not allow fear to control my home, my mind, or my parenting. God has given me power, love, and a

sound mind. My children belong ultimately to Him, and He is faithful to guide and protect them."

Prayer Against Fear

Heavenly Father,

You see every fear hidden within my heart. You know the worries I carry concerning my children, my family, and the future. Today I surrender every anxious thought into Your hands.

Forgive me for the times fear became louder than faith. Teach me to trust You deeply even when life feels uncertain. Replace panic with peace, confusion with clarity, and torment with a sound mind.

Protect my children spiritually, emotionally, physically, and mentally. Guide them when I cannot be present beside them. Surround them with Your favor, wisdom, and protection.

And Lord, help me create an atmosphere within my home filled not with fear, but with faith, peace, wisdom, and trust in Your unfailing love.

In Jesus' name, Amen.

CHAPTER 9
THE BATTLE OF COMPARISON
"When Mothers Forget Their Own Assignment"

"They measuring themselves by themselves, and comparing themselves among themselves, are not wise." — 2 Corinthians 10:12

One of the quietest battles destroying peace in modern motherhood is comparison.

It rarely announces itself loudly at first.

It enters subtly.

A mother scrolls through social media and suddenly feels inadequate.

Another child excels academically, and insecurity quietly awakines.

Someone else's family appears more spiritual, more successful, more disciplined, more beautiful, more accomplished.

And slowly, without realizing it, joy begins to disappear.

Comparison is dangerous because it shifts focus away from God's assignment toward someone else's appearance.

It causes mothers to evaluate their worth through visible outcomes instead of faithfulness.

And in today's world, comparison has become relentless.

Previous generations compared within neighborhoods.

Modern mothers compare globally every single day.

- ✓ *Perfect family photographs.*
- ✓ *Perfect vacations.*

- ✓ *Perfect homes.*
- ✓ *Perfect parenting moments.*
- ✓ *Perfect children.*
- ✓ *Perfect marriages.*
- ✓ *Perfect spirituality.*

But most of what people display publicly hides realities privately.

Comparison feeds on illusion.

Many mothers today secretly carry guilt because they believe they are failing compared to others.

They feel their children are behind.

Their homes are less organized.

Their parenting less effective.

Their finances less stable.

Their spiritual lives less impressive.

And slowly comparison steals peace, confidence, and identity.

Yet one of the greatest revelations mothers must understand is this:

God never called mothers to compete with one another.

He called them to steward their unique assignment faithfully.

Every child is different.

Every family is different.

Every journey is different.

Every season is different.

And comparison becomes destructive because it ignores individuality and uniqueness.

A mother raising a quiet, artistic child cannot parent exactly like a mother raising a bold, athletic child.

A family walking through grief cannot function exactly like a family in a season of celebration. Different assignments require different grace.

This is why comparison becomes spiritually dangerous—it tempts mothers to abandon divine wisdom in order to imitate visible trends.

And imitation without discernment creates confusion.

One of the enemy's greatest strategies is identity theft through comparison.

When mothers constantly compare, they slowly forget who they are and what God specifically entrusted to them.

They begin parenting according to pressure instead of purpose.

Some push children aggressively because they fear being *"behind."*

Others force children into achievements that match society's expectations rather than God's design.

Some become emotionally harsh because comparison created insecurity.

Others become exhausted trying to prove themselves constantly.

But comparison never produces peace.

Because there will always be someone appearing more successful externally.

This battle existed long before social media.

Even within Scripture we see how comparison wounded relationships, distorted identity, and created unnecessary pain. Rachel and Leah experienced this deeply.

Genesis reveals two sisters trapped in painful comparison for years. Leah desired Jacob's love. Rachel desired children. Each woman focused on what the other possessed rather than recognizing her own blessings.

Comparison blinded both women emotionally.

And that still happens today.

Comparison causes mothers to overlook what God is doing within their own homes because they remain distracted by someone else's story.

One mother compares children academically.

- ✓ *Another compares finances.*
- ✓ *Another compares beauty*
- ✓ *Another compares spirituality.*
- ✓ *Another compares opportunities.*

But comparison eventually produces either pride or insecurity. Neither produces peace.

Mary and Martha reveal another dimension of comparison in the New Testament.

While Martha busied herself serving, she became frustrated because Mary sat listening to Jesus.

Notice Martha's words:

"Lord, dost thou not care that my sister hath left me to serve alone?" — Luke 10:40

Comparison distorted Martha's perspective emotionally.

Instead of focusing on her own assignment, she became consumed by someone else's position. This happens constantly in parenting.

Mothers stop stewarding their own homes peacefully because they are distracted by what others are doing. Comparison creates unnecessary emotional pressure. One mother feels guilty because another homeschools successfully.

Another feels guilty because someone else's children excel academically.

Another feels ashamed because her child struggles emotionally or behaviorally.

And quietly many mothers begin asking: *"Why isn't my child like theirs?"*

But comparison ignores something deeply important:

God never creates two destinies identically. Even within Scripture, children developed differently.
Joseph dreamed.
David worshipped.
Daniel excelled administratively.
Peter led boldly.
John loved deeply.
Esther carried influence differently than Deborah.
Timothy matured differently than Paul.
Difference is not deficiency.
Yet comparison convinces mothers that uniqueness is weakness.
One of the deepest wounds comparison creates is identity confusion within children themselves. Children who are constantly compared often develop deep insecurity internally.
"Why can't you be more like your brother?"
"Look how well she performs."
"Other children behave better."
"Your cousin is more disciplined."
Comparison may temporarily motivate externally, but it often wounds identity internally.
Children begin believing love is performance-based. That acceptance depends upon achievement. That they must compete for approval.
And many adults still carry emotional scars from constant comparison during childhood.
Wise mothers understand something powerful:
Children flourish where individuality is celebrated, not constantly compared.
This does not mean standards disappear.
Correction still matters.
Growth still matters.
Responsibility still matters.

But identity must never become chained to competition.

A woman named Anita learned this lesson painfully.

Her daughter Meera struggled academically while her cousin excelled constantly. Family gatherings became emotionally difficult because relatives repeatedly praised the cousin publicly while questioning Meera's performance privately.

Without realizing it, Anita slowly began pressuring Meera harder and harder.

More tuition classes.

More criticism.

More comparison.

More frustration.

Eventually Meera became withdrawn emotionally.

One evening Anita overheard her daughter quietly telling a friend: *"No matter what I do, I'll never be enough."*

That sentence shattered Anita's heart.

She realized comparison had slowly damaged her daughter's confidence and emotional safety.

Instead of nurturing Meera's uniqueness, she had been trying to make her resemble someone else.

That night Anita prayed deeply and asked God to help her truly see her daughter again.

Over time she began noticing gifts she previously overlooked—Meera possessed remarkable compassion, creativity, emotional intelligence, and communication skills.

As Anita shifted from comparison to intentional encouragement, Meera slowly regained confidence. Years later she became highly effective in counseling and mentoring young girls emotionally.

Anita later realized something profound:

Comparison almost blinded her to the actual calling God had placed upon her child.

Many mothers today are unintentionally raising children under performance pressure rather than purpose-centered identity.

But God never evaluates people according to comparison charts.

He measures faithfulness.

This becomes especially important in the age of social media.

Social media magnifies comparison because people typically display highlights while hiding struggles. Mothers compare their private realities against someone else's edited moments. And this creates emotional exhaustion.

Some mothers feel pressured to create "perfect homes" publicly while privately drowning emotionally.

Others feel spiritually inadequate because another family appears more disciplined or visibly successful.

But appearances rarely tell complete stories.

Some of the families appearing strongest publicly may secretly struggle deeply privately.

This is why mothers must guard their hearts carefully.

Proverbs 4:23 says:

"Keep thy heart with all diligence…"

Guarding the heart includes guarding what shapes *identity, peace, and perspective.* Comparison distorts all three.

One of the enemy's goals is distracting mothers from nurturing spiritual atmosphere by trapping them in endless competition.

Comparison-focused homes often become tense homes. Performance becomes central. Children feel pressure constantly. Rest disappears. Joy weakens. And emotional connection suffers.

But purpose-centered homes feel different. Children feel seen. Known. Valued. Guided. Corrected lovingly. Encouraged intentionally.

This does not produce laziness—it produces healthy rootedness.

One of the most powerful truths mothers must remember is this:

Your assignment is not to raise someone else's child.

It is to steward the child God entrusted specifically to you. And every child carries different wiring, gifts, struggles, strengths, weaknesses, timing, and purpose.

Even Jesus developed progressively.

Luke 2:52 says: *"And Jesus increased in wisdom and stature…"*

Growth itself is process. Not every child matures identically or simultaneously.

Some bloom early. Others bloom later. Some excel publicly. Others carry quieter strengths.

Some children appear difficult because their gifting requires different nurturing.

David himself was overlooked initially by his own family. When Samuel arrived to anoint Israel's future king, David was not even invited initially.

Yet Heaven had already chosen him.

This is important because many children underestimated by society may still carry profound destiny.

Comparison blinds people to hidden greatness.

One of the deepest revelations within this chapter is this:

Comparison kills gratitude.

Mothers consumed with what others possess often stop recognizing what God has already placed within their own homes. Gratitude restores perspective.

It reminds mothers that every child is a gift, not a competition project.

Every family journey carries sacred uniqueness.

And every mother requires grace for her specific assignment.

This is why mature mothers celebrate others without diminishing themselves.

They can applaud another child's success without feeling threatened.

Another mother's strength does not cancel your worth.

Another family's blessings do not erase God's plans for your home.

Kingdom-minded mothers do not compete—they encourage one another. Because motherhood was never designed as rivalry. It was designed as stewardship.

And perhaps one of the greatest freedoms mothers can experience is this:

When comparison dies, peace returns.

Joy returns.

Connection returns.

Identity strengthens.

Children breathe emotionally again. And homes slowly become places of acceptance instead of constant pressure.

Not because excellence disappears. But because love becomes stronger than competition. And children raised within secure identity often become healthier emotionally, spiritually, and relationally for generations to come.

Reflection Questions

- ✓ *In what areas am I most tempted to compare my family with others?*
- ✓ *Has comparison stolen joy or peace from my motherhood journey?*
- ✓ *Have I unknowingly compared my children with others verbally or emotionally?*
- ✓ *What unique strengths has God placed within my children?*
- ✓ *Am I parenting through pressure or through purpose?*

Practical Action Plan

Step 1: Limit Comparison Triggers

Reduce unhealthy exposure to influences that consistently create insecurity, pressure, or discouragement.

Step 2: Celebrate Individuality

Intentionally affirm the unique strengths, personality, and gifting within each child.

Step 3: Practice Gratitude Daily

Spend time thanking God specifically for your children, your family journey, and the grace He has provided for your assignment.

Family Exercise

As a family, allow each person to share one unique strength or gift they appreciate about every other family member.

Declaration

"I will not measure my worth, my children, or my family against others. God has entrusted me with a unique assignment, and I will steward it faithfully with peace, wisdom, gratitude, and love."

Prayer Against Comparison

Heavenly Father,

Forgive me for the times comparison has stolen my peace, joy, confidence, and gratitude. Help me stop measuring my family against the lives of others. Teach me to see my children through Your eyes and not through society's expectations.

Heal every insecurity within me that causes pressure, striving, or fear. Help me nurture purpose instead of performance. Teach me to celebrate the unique gifts and timing You have placed within each child.

Remove unhealthy competition, jealousy, and discouragement from my heart and from my home. Let our family atmosphere be filled with peace, encouragement, identity, and grace.

And Lord, help me become the kind of mother who builds confidence instead of comparison, purpose instead of pressure, and love instead of performance.

In Jesus' name, Amen.

CHAPTER 10
THE BATTLE FOR THE HOME ATMOSPHERE
"Children Grow in Atmospheres Before Instruction"

"Let no corrupt communication proceed out of your mouth, but that which is good to the use of edifying..."
— Ephesians 4:29

"Train up a child in the way he should go..." — Proverbs 22:6

Long before children understand sermons, they absorb atmosphere.

Before they fully understand theology, they sense emotional climate.

Before they learn doctrine, they observe reactions, tones, tensions, conversations, and behaviors within the home.

Children grow in atmospheres before instruction.

This is one of the most overlooked truths in parenting.

Many parents focus heavily on correcting behavior while ignoring the environment shaping that behavior daily. But atmosphere is powerful.

Invisible things often shape visible outcomes.

A seed grows according to the environment surrounding it. Even healthy seeds struggle in toxic soil. In the same way, children develop emotionally, spiritually, and mentally according to the atmosphere surrounding them consistently.

Some homes carry peace. Others carry tension.

Some homes feel emotionally safe. Others feel unpredictable.

Some homes are filled with encouragement. Others with criticism.

Some homes carry spiritual hunger. Others carry emotional heaviness.

And children absorb these climates deeply.

This is why the battle for the home atmosphere matters so much.

Satan understands something many families overlook:

If he cannot destroy children directly, he will often attempt to poison the environment surrounding them.

Because atmosphere shapes identity quietly over time.

Children raised in fearful homes often become anxious.

Children raised in angry homes often become emotionally defensive.

Children raised in peaceful homes often develop emotional stability.

Children raised in spiritually alive homes often become spiritually sensitive.

Atmosphere teaches continuously—even when nobody is speaking intentionally.

This is why mothers carry tremendous influence within the home. Mothers often become emotional thermostats within families. Their words, reactions, emotional health, spiritual consistency, and daily habits significantly affect the climate children experience.

This does not mean fathers are unimportant. But Scripture repeatedly reveals the unusual influence mothers carry in shaping emotional and spiritual foundations.

One of the deepest revelations mothers must understand is this:

Children may forget many instructions—but they rarely forget atmospheres.

A child may not remember every Bible lesson taught formally, but they will remember: *Whether the home felt safe.*

Whether peace existed.

Whether prayer happened naturally.

Whether anger dominated conversations.

Whether love felt consistent.

Whether parents honored one another.

Whether fear or faith ruled the home.

Atmosphere becomes memory. And memory shapes identity.

This is why Deuteronomy 6 describes spiritual teaching not merely as formal instruction, but as daily atmosphere:

"And thou shalt teach them diligently unto thy children, and shalt talk of them when thou sittest in thine house…"

God intended truth to live within daily family culture—not merely within occasional religious activities.

Some parents want godly children while creating atmospheres that constantly contradict godly values.

Children hear Scripture quoted publicly but experience chaos privately.

They hear *"God is peace*" while the home remains filled with shouting, criticism, hostility, fear, or emotional coldness. Eventually children become confused. Because atmosphere often speaks louder than instruction.

This is why authenticity matters deeply.

A praying mother does not simply teach truth. She cultivates environments where truth becomes livable.

Jesus Himself understood the power of atmosphere. Children were drawn naturally toward Him. Broken people felt safe near Him.

Peace surrounded His presence even during storms. And homes influenced by Christ should increasingly reflect His atmosphere too.

Not perfect homes. But healing homes.

Peaceful homes. Truth-filled homes.

Homes where repentance exists.

Homes where forgiveness happens.

Homes where prayer feels natural rather than forced.

One of the greatest battles modern families face is emotional exhaustion within the home atmosphere.

Busy schedules.

Digital distractions.

Financial pressures.

Stress.

Overstimulation.

Constant noise.

Emotional burnout.

Many homes today function efficiently externally while suffering emotionally internally.

People live together physically while disconnected relationally.

Conversations become transactional instead of meaningful. Devices become louder than relationships. And spiritual atmosphere weakens gradually.

The enemy understands that distracted homes often become spiritually vulnerable homes. This is why mothers must intentionally guard atmosphere.

Atmosphere never develops accidentally.

It develops intentionally or unintentionally.

A home filled continually with anger, negativity, gossip, disrespect, fear, or emotional instability will eventually shape children accordingly.
But homes intentionally cultivated with peace, honor, truth, prayer, joy, forgiveness, and love create emotional safety where children flourish.
The Old Testament provides powerful examples of atmosphere shaping generations.
Joshua declared:
"As for me and my house, we will serve the Lord." — Joshua 24:15
Notice the language of household culture. Not occasional spirituality. Lifestyle atmosphere. The home itself became dedicated ground.
Samuel also grew within spiritual atmosphere because Hannah intentionally connected him to God's presence from childhood.
Though Eli's household carried corruption, Samuel had already been planted spiritually through his mother's prayers and dedication.
This reveals something powerful:
Children anchored early spiritually can survive unhealthy environments later more effectively.
Invisible foundations matter deeply.
Timothy's story reveals this beautifully in the New Testament.
Paul reminds Timothy of the *"unfeigned faith"* that first lived in his grandmother Lois and his mother Eunice. Faith became generational atmosphere before it became personal conviction. This is profoundly important.
Children often inherit spiritual atmosphere long before developing mature faith personally.
Homes filled with prayer normalize dependence upon God.

Homes filled with worship normalize God's presence.
Homes filled with forgiveness normalize grace.
Homes filled with honor normalize respect.
And homes filled with emotional instability normalize dysfunction.
Children absorb what surrounds them repeatedly.
A woman named Deborah learned this lesson painfully.
Her home appeared successful externally. Her children attended good schools. The family remained financially stable. Activities filled every week.
But internally the home atmosphere had become emotionally tense.
Her husband remained constantly stressed from work.
Deborah herself carried unresolved exhaustion and frustration. Conversations became sharp. Meals became rushed. Prayer disappeared gradually. Everyone spent increasing time isolated on devices.
One evening her young daughter Sophia asked quietly: *"Why does our house always feel angry?"*
That question deeply convicted Deborah. She realized something important:
Her family did not merely need better schedules. They needed a healthier atmosphere.
Over the following months Deborah intentionally began reshaping the home environment.
Not perfectly. But intentionally.
She reduced unnecessary busyness.
Created technology-free family evenings.
Began praying openly with the children again.
Played worship music regularly.
Spoke more gently intentionally.
Started blessing family members verbally.
Encouraged honest conversations emotionally.

Slowly the atmosphere shifted.
Tension lessened.
Connection deepened.
Peace increased.
Years later Sophia reflected: *"Our house changed when Mom changed the atmosphere."*
One of the deepest revelations in this chapter is this:
Atmosphere is built repeatedly through small daily patterns.
Not grand occasional moments.
Daily words.
Daily reactions.
Daily routines.
Daily emotional responses.
Daily spiritual habits.
Children grow inside these repeated environments.
This is why words matter profoundly.
Proverbs 18:21 says: *"Death and life are in the power of the tongue…"*
Words carry spiritual and emotional weight.
A home constantly filled with criticism, sarcasm, shouting, or negativity creates emotional heaviness. But homes filled with encouragement, blessing, patience, and truth create emotional strength.
Many mothers underestimate how deeply children internalize repeated tones and phrases. Some children grow up constantly bracing emotionally because anger dominates the atmosphere.
Others grow rooted confidently because peace consistently surrounds them.
This does not mean conflict never happens in healthy homes.
Every family experiences difficult moments. But healthy atmospheres know how to repair after conflict.

Apologies happen.
Forgiveness happens.
Healing conversations happen.
Children do not need perfect parents. They need emotionally honest and spiritually healthy environments.
One of the enemy's greatest strategies is normalizing toxic atmospheres.
Constant yelling becomes "normal." Emotional distance becomes "normal."
Disrespect becomes "normal." Prayerlessness becomes "normal."
But what becomes normal eventually becomes generational.
This is why praying mothers must become atmosphere protectors. Not controlling every detail obsessively. But intentionally cultivating what enters and remains within the home spiritually and emotionally.
Music matters.
Conversations matter.
Media matters.
Tone matters.
Honor matters.
Emotional consistency matters.
Spiritual rhythms matter.
Many mothers pray for children while unknowingly tolerating atmospheres that weaken spiritual health daily. But atmosphere either nourishes or drains spiritual growth.
This becomes especially important regarding emotional climate.
Children should not feel they must constantly walk on emotional eggshells within their own home.
Fearful atmospheres damage emotional security.

A child uncertain whether parents will respond with explosive anger, harsh criticism, or emotional withdrawal often develops anxiety internally.
Peaceful homes create emotional safety where children can grow honestly.
This is why James 1:19 remains so important: *"Let every man be swift to hear, slow to speak, slow to wrath."*
Peaceful atmospheres require emotional maturity. Mothers must learn to process stress without releasing constant emotional pressure onto the home.
This does not mean suppressing emotions artificially.
It means surrendering emotions healthily before God.
One of the greatest gifts mothers can give children is emotional stability.
Not emotional perfection. But stability.
Children thrive where consistency exists.
Where love remains dependable.
Where correction happens without humiliation.
Where mistakes become opportunities for growth rather than fear.
Another critical part of atmosphere is spiritual environment.
Some homes mention God occasionally. Others cultivate awareness of His presence regularly.
Simple habits shape spiritual climate powerfully:

- ✓ *Prayer before school*
- ✓ *Worship during ordinary moments*
- ✓ *Scripture conversations naturally*
- ✓ *Blessing children verbally*
- ✓ *Gratitude practices*
- ✓ *Family prayer times*
- ✓ *Speaking faith during difficult seasons*

These moments may seem small individually. But together they create spiritual culture.
Culture shapes identity. And identity shapes generations.
One of the most powerful truths mothers must remember is this:
Children often become what atmospheres repeatedly reinforce.
If children repeatedly experience peace, honor, love, prayer, forgiveness, truth, and encouragement, those values become internalized deeply. This does not guarantee perfection.
Every child still possesses free will. But healthy atmosphere builds strong invisible foundations. And perhaps that is why Satan fights homes so aggressively.
Because strong atmospheres produce resilient generations.
Generations able to survive cultural pressure.
Generations emotionally secure.
Generations spiritually rooted.
Generations capable of hearing God amid confusion.
One praying mother intentionally protecting atmosphere can change the future of an entire family line. Because atmosphere today becomes legacy tomorrow.

Reflection Questions

- ✓ *What emotional atmosphere currently exists within my home?*
- ✓ *Do my children experience peace or tension most consistently?*
- ✓ *What words are spoken most often within our family?*

- ✓ *Is our home spiritually alive or spiritually distracted?*
- ✓ *What atmosphere patterns need healing or intentional change?*

Practical Action Plan

Step 1: Evaluate the Home Atmosphere Honestly

Pay attention to recurring emotional patterns, communication styles, stress levels, and spiritual habits within the home.

Step 2: Establish Life-Giving Rhythms

Create regular moments for prayer, encouragement, worship, gratitude, and healthy conversation.

Step 3: Guard What Enters the Home

Evaluate media, music, conversations, and influences that shape emotional and spiritual climate daily.

Family Exercise

Choose one evening each week as a "*Peace & Presence Night.*" Turn off distractions, worship together briefly, pray together, share gratitude, and speak blessings over one another.

Declaration

"My home will become a place of peace, healing, truth, prayer, honor, and emotional safety. My children will grow in an atmosphere that strengthens their identity, faith, and future."

Prayer for the Home Atmosphere

Heavenly Father,

Thank You for entrusting my home and family into my care. Forgive me for every way unhealthy atmosphere may have entered our home through

fear, anger, stress, harshness, negativity, or spiritual neglect.
Teach me how to cultivate peace, wisdom, gentleness, truth, and spiritual life within our family. Let Your presence fill our home. Remove every atmosphere of confusion, emotional heaviness, division, bitterness, and fear.
Help me use my words to build and not destroy. Teach our family how to communicate with honor, patience, and love. Restore emotional safety where wounds have formed.
May our home become a place where Your presence is welcomed, where prayer is natural, where healing flows, and where future generations are strengthened spiritually and emotionally.
And Lord, let the atmosphere within our home become fertile ground for destiny, faith, wisdom, and godly legacy.
In Jesus' name, Amen.

PART 3

THE REWARD OF A PRAYING MOTHER

CHAPTER 11
DOUBLE HONOUR
"God Restores What Tears Once Watered"

"For your shame ye shall have double…"
— Isaiah 61:7

There are seasons in a mother's life when sacrifice feels invisible.
Years of prayer.
Years of serving.
Years of giving emotionally.
Years of waiting silently.
Years of crying privately.
Years of carrying burdens others never fully understood.
Many mothers pour out their strength into families while receiving little recognition publicly. Their prayers happen in hidden places. Their sacrifices often go unnoticed. Their emotional battles remain invisible to others.
But Heaven never overlooks hidden faithfulness.
One of the greatest revelations throughout Scripture is this:
God remembers praying mothers. Not occasionally. Completely!

- ✓ *Every tear.*
- ✓ *Every prayer.*
- ✓ *Every sleepless night.*
- ✓ *Every hidden sacrifice.*
- ✓ *Every act of faithfulness.*

Nothing escapes Heaven's attention. And in God's kingdom, hidden obedience eventually produces visible reward.

This does not always happen according to human timing. But throughout Scripture we repeatedly see a divine principle:

God restores faithfully surrendered pain.

Isaiah 61:7 declares: *"For your shame ye shall have double..."*

What a remarkable promise. Not merely restoration. Double restoration.

God specializes in restoring what grief, delay, warfare, disappointment, betrayal, and suffering attempted to destroy.

This chapter is deeply important because many mothers secretly wonder whether their sacrifices truly matter.

Some prayed for years without visible change.

Some carried families through storms silently.

Some endured loneliness, rejection, abandonment, or emotional exhaustion.

Some sowed faithfully into children who temporarily wandered far from God.

And many quietly ask: *"Will my prayers ever bear fruit?"*

Scripture answers clearly: Yes. God is not unjust to forget faithfulness.

Galatians 6:9 reminds us: *"In due season we shall reap, if we faint not."*

Due season exists. And one of the enemy's greatest strategies is convincing mothers to stop believing before harvest appears. But praying mothers must understand something powerful:

Seeds buried are not seeds forgotten. Many answers develop invisibly long before manifestation becomes visible.

Farmers understand this principle deeply. After sowing, there is often silence before growth appears. But silence does not mean inactivity.

Roots develop underground before fruit emerges above ground. And prayer often works the same way.

Some mothers are standing today in "underground seasons" where Heaven is still working invisibly. Yet Scripture repeatedly reveals that God eventually brings hidden faithfulness into visible testimony.

Hannah's life demonstrates this beautifully.

For years Hannah carried shame publicly because of barrenness. Her tears became constant companions. Peninnah mocked her repeatedly. Her pain became so deep that even Eli misunderstood her anguish initially.

But Hannah continued bringing her sorrow before God honestly. And eventually God answered. Not only did Hannah receive Samuel—God later blessed her with additional children as well.

What began as humiliation became honor.

What began as tears became testimony.

And perhaps one of the deepest revelations in Hannah's story is this:

God often restores publicly what was suffered privately.

The same woman once mocked for barrenness eventually became known as the mother of a prophet who transformed Israel spiritually.

Imagine Hannah watching Samuel grow into his calling.

Imagine hearing him speak God's voice nationally.

Imagine realizing her tears helped shape a generation.
A mother's prayer outlives her lifetime.
Many mothers pray for immediate relief without realizing Heaven is building generational impact.
Hannah prayed for a child. God raised a prophet. The reward exceeded the request.
This is often God's pattern. He answers beyond what people initially imagine.
Job's story reveals another powerful principle of restoration.
Though Job's story centers largely around personal suffering, the restoration principle applies deeply here:
"So the Lord blessed the latter end of Job more than his beginning…" — Job 42:12
Notice something important.
God did not merely restore what Job lost. He expanded restoration.
This reveals God's heart toward surrendered suffering.
The enemy desires pain to end in destruction. God desires surrendered pain to end in redemption.
Many mothers fear painful seasons permanently ruined their families, children, or futures. But God specializes in rebuilding what looked impossible to restore.
Some mothers reading this chapter feel emotionally weary because they have sown faithfully for years while seeing little visible fruit.
Children remain distant.
Prayers remain unanswered.
Family wounds remain unresolved.
But Scripture repeatedly teaches that faithfulness matters even during invisible seasons.

One of the greatest lies mothers believe is: *"If I do not see immediate results, nothing is happening."*
But God frequently works progressively.
Process does not mean absence.
Seeds require time.
Healing requires time.
Restoration requires time.
Growth requires time.
Even Jesus developed progressively. Luke 2:52 says: *"And Jesus increased…"*
Growth itself is process.
One of the most beautiful truths mothers must remember is this:
God rewards faithfulness, not merely visible outcomes.
The world celebrates visible success. God honors surrendered obedience.
A mother praying quietly for her family carries eternal significance even when public recognition never arrives immediately.
Heaven values hidden intercession deeply.
Some of the greatest spiritual victories in history were birthed through unseen prayers from faithful mothers.
Monica prayed persistently for Augustine long before he became one of Christianity's most influential voices.
At one point Augustine lived rebelliously, rejecting the faith his mother taught him. Many people would have given up emotionally. But Monica persevered.
Years later Augustine surrendered fully to God, and history itself changed through the influence of a praying mother.
Her tears outlived her lifetime. This is profoundly important.

Praying mothers often influence generations they may never fully see personally.

One prayer can affect grandchildren not yet born.

One faithful atmosphere can alter entire family patterns.

One surrendered life can reverse generational destruction.

This is why the enemy fights praying mothers aggressively. Because he understands their influence reaches far beyond one moment.

A woman named Esther experienced this reality personally.

After her husband abandoned the family unexpectedly, Esther spent years raising her children alone. Financial pressure became intense. Emotional exhaustion became constant. There were seasons she questioned whether her prayers truly mattered.

Her oldest son Caleb became deeply rebellious during his teenage years. Anger consumed him. He blamed God for the pain their family endured. Eventually he distanced himself emotionally and spiritually.

Many nights Esther cried herself to sleep praying for restoration.

Years passed.

Sometimes hope weakened.

Sometimes faith felt exhausted.

Yet she continued praying.

Not perfectly. But persistently.

Slowly small changes began emerging.

Caleb eventually encountered godly mentors who challenged his bitterness. Conversations with his mother gradually reopened emotionally. Healing unfolded through process.

Years later Caleb became actively involved in helping young men from broken families.

One evening during a church gathering he publicly honored his mother and said: *"My mother's prayers carried me when I was too broken to carry myself."*

Esther realized something deeply moving in that moment:

The tears she once cried privately had become public testimony.

This is often how God works.

Pain surrendered faithfully eventually becomes witness.

And one of the most beautiful rewards for praying mothers is not merely external blessing—it is watching restoration unfold where destruction once threatened.

Yet this chapter must also address an important truth honestly:

Double honor does not always mean life becomes easy.

Some mothers assume restoration means the absence of future pain entirely. But biblical restoration often means redeemed purpose, renewed peace, deeper strength, spiritual fruitfulness, and lasting impact despite previous suffering.

Joseph still carried memories of betrayal after restoration.

David still remembered painful seasons.

Paul still carried scars.

But redeemed pain no longer controlled their identity.

Likewise many mothers may still remember difficult years emotionally. But restored mothers no longer live imprisoned by those seasons.

God transforms wounds into wisdom. Tears into authority.

Pain into compassion. Brokenness into ministry.
One of the deepest revelations in this chapter is this: Heaven measures reward differently than earth.
Some mothers seek validation from people who may never fully understand their sacrifices.
But God sees differently.
Jesus taught repeatedly that hidden faithfulness matters eternally.
"Thy Father which seeth in secret himself shall reward thee openly." — Matthew 6:4
Secret prayers matter.
Secret tears matter.
Secret obedience matters.
Secret surrender matters.
Nothing offered to God faithfully remains wasted.
And often the greatest earthly reward a praying mother experiences is not material blessing—but transformed generations.
Watching children healed emotionally.
Watching prodigals return.
Watching families restored.
Watching grandchildren raised within godly legacy.
Watching cycles of addiction, abuse, fear, or dysfunction broken permanently.
This is double honor. Because what once threatened destruction becomes testimony of redemption.
This does not happen through human strength alone. It happens through surrendered partnership with God over time.
One of the most healing truths mothers must embrace is this:
Your current season is not your final chapter.
Some mothers feel trapped in painful present circumstances and assume nothing will ever change.
But Scripture repeatedly proves otherwise.

Naomi's bitterness was not final.
Hannah's barrenness was not final.
Elizabeth's delay was not final.
Peter's failure was not final.
Thomas' doubt was not final.
And your present pain is not final either.
God still restores.
Still heals.
Still rebuilds.
Still redeems.
Still honors surrendered faithfulness.
And perhaps one of the most powerful truths in this chapter is this:
Praying mothers may feel forgotten by people temporarily—but they are never forgotten by God.
Every whispered prayer.
Every exhausted worship song.
Every midnight cry.
Every fast.
Every act of forgiveness.
Every sacrifice.
Every moment of perseverance.
Heaven remembers all of it. And at the appointed time, God brings beauty from ashes.
Not because mothers were perfect. But because they remained surrendered.
And generations often rise later because one mother refused to stop praying.

Reflection Questions

- ✓ *What painful season am I still waiting for God to restore?*
- ✓ *Have I mistaken delay for abandonment?*
- ✓ *What hidden sacrifices have I offered faithfully before God?*

- ✓ *Where have I already seen signs of God's restoration?*
- ✓ *What generational cycles am I believing God to break through my prayers?*

Practical Action Plan

Step 1: Remember God's Past Faithfulness

Write down testimonies, answered prayers, and moments where God sustained you previously.

Step 2: Continue Sowing Faithfully

Do not stop praying, blessing, nurturing, and believing even when visible harvest seems delayed.

Step 3: Speak Restoration Over Your Family

Declare God's promises over broken areas instead of partnering with hopelessness.

Family Exercise

As a family, share testimonies of how God has brought healing, provision, restoration, or breakthrough during difficult seasons.

Declaration

"My tears are not wasted. God remembers every prayer, every sacrifice, and every act of faithfulness. Shame will not define my story. God is bringing restoration, healing, and generational blessing from every surrendered season."

Prayer for Double Honour

Heavenly Father,

Thank You for seeing every hidden sacrifice, every silent prayer, and every tear I have poured before You. When others did not understand my pain, You remained near.

Today I surrender every broken dream, every disappointment, every delay, and every wounded place into Your hands again. Restore what sorrow attempted to destroy. Heal what grief weakened. Rebuild what fear damaged.
Lord, let my family experience Your redemption. Let prodigals return, wounded hearts heal, broken relationships restore, and generational cycles break through Your power.
Teach me to trust Your timing even when I cannot yet see the full harvest. Strengthen me to remain faithful during hidden seasons. And may my prayers continue producing fruit long after my lifetime.
For every season of shame, discouragement, loneliness, and tears, release Your double honor, peace, healing, and restoration according to Your will.
In Jesus' name, Amen.

CHAPTER 12
GENERATIONAL LEGACY
"When a Mother's Prayer Outlives Her Lifetime"

"I call to remembrance the unfeigned faith that is in thee, which dwelt first in thy grandmother Lois, and thy mother Eunice…"
— 2 Timothy 1:5

"His seed shall be mighty upon earth: the generation of the upright shall be blessed." — Psalm 112:2

One of the greatest misconceptions about motherhood is the belief that a mother's influence ends when her physical presence ends.

But Scripture reveals something far deeper.

A praying mother never dies completely.

Her words remain.

Her prayers remain.

Her atmosphere remains.

Her values remain.

Her spiritual deposits remain.

And often, long after her voice becomes silent on earth, the seeds she planted continue producing fruit across generations. This is the mystery of generational legacy.

God designed motherhood not merely for raising children temporarily, but for shaping future generations spiritually, emotionally, and morally.

A mother may never stand behind a pulpit.

May never become famous publicly.

May never lead globally.

Yet through prayer, atmosphere, and faithful influence, she may shape generations she will never personally meet.

This is holy influence. And Satan fights it fiercely because he understands something many mothers underestimate:

Healthy generations rarely happen accidentally.

They are usually built intentionally through hidden faithfulness over time.

The enemy understands that if he can weaken mothers spiritually, emotionally, or morally, he can weaken future generations simultaneously.

Because mothers often shape invisible foundations long before visible outcomes appear. This is why the battle over motherhood is ultimately a battle over legacy.

Psalm 112 declares: *"The generation of the upright shall be blessed."*

Notice the language of generational impact.

God thinks beyond individuals. He thinks in generations.

One surrendered life can affect countless future lives.

One praying mother can interrupt destructive family cycles that existed for decades.

One spiritually healthy home can become a refuge for generations.

And perhaps one of the deepest revelations in this entire book is this:

Children inherit far more than genetics.

They inherit atmospheres.

Mindsets.

Patterns.

Emotional responses.

Spiritual habits.

Beliefs.

Values.
Unresolved wounds.
Or healed wisdom.

Generations carry what previous generations cultivated or tolerated.

This is why praying mothers matter so profoundly. Because prayer can interrupt inherited destruction.

Some families inherit addiction patterns.
Others inherit rage.
Others inherit fear.
Others inherit emotional distance.
Others inherit divorce cycles.
Others inherit poverty thinking.
Others inherit spiritual compromise.

But through surrendered prayer and intentional living, mothers can become generational turning points.

The story changes with them.

The cycle ends with them.

This is deeply important because many mothers today feel overwhelmed by the brokenness surrounding them.

Some were never raised in healthy homes themselves.

Some never experienced emotional safety personally.

Some inherited trauma, dysfunction, abandonment, or instability.

And secretly they fear: *"What if I repeat what I came from?"*

But the Gospel is deeply generational in power. Jesus does not merely save individuals.

He transforms legacies.

A praying mother may have inherited brokenness, yet through God's healing she can establish an entirely different foundation for future generations.

This is redemption at work.
Lois and Eunice reveal this beautifully in Scripture.
Paul tells Timothy that sincere faith first lived in his grandmother Lois and his mother Eunice before becoming established in Timothy himself.
Notice the order. Faith became generational before it became personal. This is profoundly powerful.
Timothy did not encounter truth accidentally.
He grew within an atmosphere where faith lived consistently. His grandmother carried it.
His mother reinforced it. And eventually Timothy embodied it personally.
What one generation protects spiritually often becomes strength for the next generation.
This is why atmosphere matters deeply.
Children may temporarily resist values. But seeds planted consistently often remain hidden within them far longer than parents realize.
Many adults later return to truths they first encountered within godly homes.
A praying mother's influence often resurfaces decades later during moments of crisis, decision, pain, or spiritual awakening. Because spiritual seeds remain alive beneath the surface.
Moses experienced this reality.
Though raised within Pharaoh's palace eventually, his earliest foundation came through Jochebed. She had only limited time physically with him during his early years, yet those early spiritual impressions shaped him profoundly enough that later he identified with God's people rather than Egypt's system.
Never underestimate early spiritual deposits.
A mother's words spoken during childhood may echo within children for decades.

The prayers whispered over sleeping children may protect them years later during unseen battles.

The worship filling a home may remain hidden within memory until adulthood.

A mother's influence stretches farther than she often realizes.

A woman named Grace understood this only later in life.

Grace spent years praying for her children and grandchildren quietly. She was not highly educated. She never held important positions publicly. Much of her life seemed ordinary externally.

But she possessed unusual consistency spiritually.

Every morning her children woke hearing worship music softly playing from the kitchen. Every night she prayed aloud over family members by name. Scriptures filled the walls of the home. Gratitude shaped conversations naturally.

Sometimes her children rolled their eyes during teenage years.

Sometimes they seemed uninterested spiritually.

Sometimes Grace wondered privately whether anything she did truly mattered.

Years later her grandson Daniel moved far away for university studies. During his first year he encountered intense emotional struggles, loneliness, and unhealthy influences. One evening while sitting alone in deep confusion emotionally, he suddenly remembered hearing his grandmother pray repeatedly throughout childhood:

"Lord, let my grandchildren never run too far to hear Your voice."

That memory pierced him deeply. He eventually returned to God fully. Years later Daniel became involved in mentoring young people spiritually, and he often said:

"My grandmother's prayers reached me long after her voice was gone."

That is generational legacy. Not temporary influence. Enduring influence.

A praying mother may leave far more behind than money, property, or achievements.

She may leave spiritual inheritance.

And spiritual inheritance outlasts material inheritance.

Many parents work tirelessly to prepare financial inheritance for children while neglecting spiritual inheritance entirely.

But Scripture repeatedly emphasizes spiritual legacy.

David declared:

"One generation shall praise thy works to another…"

— Psalm 145:4

God intended truth to travel across generations. Not merely through churches. But through homes.

This is why the enemy aggressively attacks family structures, spiritual disciplines, emotional health, and parental influence.

Because he understands something deeply important:

Strong generations threaten darkness.

Children raised within godly atmosphere become spiritually resilient.

Children taught prayer develop spiritual reflexes during crisis.

Children raised with truth possess anchors during cultural confusion.

Children who witness authentic faith develop discernment.

This does not guarantee children never struggle or wander temporarily.
Even biblical families experienced painful seasons.
But healthy spiritual foundations increase resilience tremendously.
One of the deepest pains many mothers carry is regret.
Regret over failures.
Regret over mistakes.
Regret over seasons they parented wounded.
Regret over words spoken harshly.
Regret over missed opportunities.
But one of the enemy's greatest traps is convincing mothers their mistakes permanently destroyed future legacy. Yet Scripture repeatedly reveals God's ability to redeem imperfect people.
Noah had failures.
David had failures.
Peter had failures.
Yet God still worked redemptively through surrendered lives.
Mothers must understand something healing:
Perfect mothers do not create godly legacies. Surrendered mothers do.
Mothers willing to repent.
Grow.
Heal.
Learn.
Pray.
Adjust.
And continue pursuing God sincerely.
Children do not need flawless mothers.
They need authentic ones.

One of the greatest gifts mothers can give future generations is emotional and spiritual healing within themselves.

Because unhealed wounds often become inherited wounds.

A mother carrying unresolved rage may unintentionally pass emotional instability forward. A mother carrying deep insecurity may unknowingly raise fearful children. But healed mothers create healthier legacies.

This is why God often heals mothers during the parenting process itself.

Sometimes while mothers pray for children, God simultaneously transforms the mother internally.

Prayer changes both generations.

One of the most beautiful truths about generational legacy is this:

Children often remember ordinary faithfulness more than extraordinary moments.

Simple prayers.

Consistent love.

Peaceful atmosphere.

Integrity.

Encouragement.

Forgiveness.

Humility.

Steady faith during difficult seasons.

These things shape identity deeply.

Many mothers underestimate small repeated acts of faithfulness because society celebrates dramatic success publicly.

But Heaven values consistency profoundly.

A child repeatedly hearing:

"God is faithful."

"Let us pray."

"We forgive."
"We trust God."
"You are loved."
"You belong to God."
These words become internal foundations over time.
One of the most powerful examples of generational legacy appears in Abraham's story.
God repeatedly spoke about Abraham's descendants.
Not merely Abraham personally.
Why? Because covenant thinking is generational.
God always sees beyond immediate moments.
And mothers must learn to think generationally too.
Not merely: *"How do I survive today?"*
But: *"What am I establishing for future generations?"*
Every atmosphere creates inheritance.
Every repeated pattern creates inheritance.
Every prayer creates inheritance.
Every spiritual discipline creates inheritance.
And every surrendered tear carries potential far beyond present visibility.
Perhaps this is why Psalm 126 says: *"They that sow in tears shall reap in joy."*
Tears are seeds.
Prayers are seeds.
Faithfulness is seed.
And seeds multiply beyond one lifetime.
One praying mother may never fully see the extent of her influence while alive on earth.
But Heaven sees completely.
Some prayers will protect children years later.
Some prayers will affect grandchildren not yet born.
Some prayers will interrupt future disasters unseen presently.

Some prayers will raise leaders, reformers, pastors, teachers, peacemakers, and healers.

Never underestimate hidden intercession.

One mother kneeling beside a bed may shape history invisibly.

One grandmother praying faithfully may alter an entire family line spiritually.

One surrendered woman may become the spiritual gatekeeper through whom future generations encounter God.

This is why motherhood is sacred. Not because mothers are perfect.

But because God entrusts eternal influence into human hands.

And perhaps one of the most comforting revelations in this chapter is this:

A praying mother's earthly life may end someday—but her prayers continue speaking long after she is gone.

Because seeds outlive sowers. And godly legacy continues long after funerals end.

Reflection Questions

- ✓ *What kind of legacy am I building within my family currently?*
- ✓ *What patterns or cycles need to stop with me?*
- ✓ *What spiritual habits am I modeling consistently before my children?*
- ✓ *What do I hope future generations will remember about my life?*
- ✓ *Am I building merely for today, or am I thinking generationally?*

Practical Action Plan

Step 1: Establish Spiritual Rhythms

Create consistent habits of prayer, worship, Scripture reading, blessing, and gratitude within the home.

Step 2: Heal Personal Wounds

Invite God to heal unresolved emotional pain that could negatively affect future generations.

Step 3: Speak Generational Blessings

Pray intentionally not only for children, but also for future grandchildren and generations yet unborn.

Family Exercise

Create a "Family Legacy Night." Share testimonies, family values, answered prayers, lessons learned, and Scriptures that the family wants future generations to remember.

Declaration

"My life will produce generational blessing. Through prayer, healing, faithfulness, and God's grace, destructive cycles will end and godly legacy will continue through my children and future generations."

Prayer for Generational Legacy

Heavenly Father,

Thank You for entrusting future generations into my influence. Help me build a legacy rooted in truth, prayer, love, healing, and faithfulness. Let my life become fertile ground for future generations to encounter You deeply.

Break every destructive cycle operating within my family line. Let patterns of fear, addiction, anger, division, compromise, and emotional brokenness end through the power of Jesus Christ.

Teach me how to model authentic faith consistently before my children. Heal every wounded place within me so I do not pass pain forward unnecessarily. Let peace, wisdom, honor, integrity, and spiritual hunger flow through our family line.

Lord, may my prayers continue speaking long after my earthly life ends. Let my children, grandchildren, and generations yet unborn walk in truth, purpose, wisdom, and the fear of the Lord.

And may my home become a testimony that one surrendered life can change generations forever.

In Jesus' name, Amen.

FINAL CHAPTER
"A MOTHER'S PRAYER NEVER FALLS TO THE GROUND"
"The Tears Heaven Refuses to Ignore"

"…for the Lord is a God of knowledge, and by him actions are weighed."
— 1 Samuel 2:3

"Thou tellest my wanderings: put thou my tears into thy bottle…" — Psalm 56:8
There are prayers spoken so softly that nobody on earth hears them except God.
Whispers released into pillows soaked with tears.
Midnight cries uttered beside sleeping children.
Silent groanings from exhausted mothers carrying burdens too deep for words.
Moments where faith trembles but refuses to die.
Moments where mothers kneel not because they are strong—but because they have nowhere else to go.
And perhaps one of the greatest revelations this book must leave within every mother's heart is this:
A mother's prayer never falls to the ground.
People may overlook it.
Children may not understand it immediately.
The world may never applaud it.
But Heaven records it.
Every tear.
Every whisper.
Every fast.
Every moment of surrender.
Every exhausted prayer prayed through heartbreak.
Nothing offered sincerely before God is wasted.

This final chapter is not merely a conclusion. It is a prophetic reminder.
A holy reassurance. A spiritual embrace for every weary mother who has ever wondered: *"Does any of this matter?"*
Yes.
It matters more than you realize. Because Heaven measures differently than earth.
Earth celebrates visible achievement. Heaven honors hidden faithfulness.
One mother kneeling in prayer may be shaping destinies more powerfully than public platforms ever could.
This is the mystery of spiritual influence.
Invisible things often carry eternal weight.
Throughout Scripture, we repeatedly see how God responds to surrendered tears.
Hannah wept before Samuel was born.
Jochebed cried before Moses delivered Israel.
Mary carried sorrow before resurrection glory appeared.
The Syrophoenician mother pressed through rejection before breakthrough came.
Monica prayed through years of rebellion before Augustine encountered Christ.
Again and again Scripture reveals the same pattern:
God remembers praying mothers.
Not one prayer escapes His attention.
Psalm 56:8 gives one of the most tender pictures in all of Scripture: *"Put thou my tears into thy bottle…"*
Imagine that.
God collects tears. Not because He enjoys pain. But because tears matter to Him.
Especially tears surrendered through faith.

There are tears of bitterness. Tears of frustration. Tears of disappointment. But there are also holy tears. Tears planted like seeds before God. And heaven never ignores surrendered tears.

One of the deepest lies Satan whispers to mothers is this: *"Nothing is changing."*

"You are wasting your prayers."

"Your children are too far gone."

"You failed."

"It is too late."

But Satan has always attacked seeds before harvest appears.

Because seeds buried underground look lifeless temporarily.

Yet hidden beneath the surface, something sacred is developing.

Prayer often works invisibly before it works visibly. And mothers must understand this deeply:

Silence does not mean absence. Delay does not mean denial. Process does not mean abandonment.

God often answers mothers through unfolding journeys rather than instant miracles.

Why? Because God is not merely raising children.

He is shaping generations. And generational transformation rarely happens overnight.

Many mothers pray for immediate rescue while God is building lasting restoration.

Many want quick change while God develops deep roots.

Roots matter because shallow foundations cannot survive storms.

This is why some of the greatest answers to prayer happen progressively.

Peter was not transformed instantly.

Joseph was not elevated instantly.

David was not crowned instantly.
Even Jesus matured progressively according to Luke 2:52.
Growth itself is process. And mothers must not despise slow transformation.
Some prayers are answered quietly over years.
A softened heart.
A restored conversation.
A child returning gradually toward God.
An emotional wound slowly healing.
A destructive cycle finally ending.
These are holy miracles too.
One of the most beautiful truths about prayer is this:
Prayer reaches where parenting cannot.
There are doors mothers cannot enter physically.
School hallways.
College dormitories.
Hidden struggles.
Private battles.
Moments of temptation.
Conversations beyond parental reach.
But prayer enters places human control never can. A mother may not know every detail her child faces. But God knows completely. And prayer invites Heaven into situations impossible to manage naturally. This is why praying mothers carry unusual spiritual authority. Not because they are perfect. But because love fuels intercession deeply.
A mother's cry before God often carries extraordinary persistence because it flows from covenant love. And covenant prayers possess enduring power.
Children may wander geographically. Emotionally. Spiritually. Morally.
But seeds remain alive.

This is one of the greatest hopes praying mothers must hold onto.
Seeds remain alive.
The enemy wants mothers to interpret temporary wandering as permanent destruction.
But throughout Scripture we see God pursuing people through years, deserts, failures, rebellion, and brokenness.
Jonah ran.
Peter failed.
Thomas doubted.
The prodigal son wandered.
Yet God still pursued. Because grace travels farther than human weakness.
Many mothers reading this book carry pain over children currently far from God.
Some feel guilt.
Some feel fear.
Some feel exhausted emotionally.
Some secretly wonder whether they failed completely.
But one of the most healing revelations mothers must embrace is this:
God loves your children even more than you do.
And His pursuit continues even when you cannot see it visibly.
Never underestimate seeds planted faithfully over years.
Scripture taught repeatedly.
Worship filling the home.
Blessings spoken over children.
Tears poured out secretly.
Godly atmosphere cultivated consistently.
These things remain alive beneath the surface far longer than mothers realize.

A woman named Ruth experienced this truth deeply. Her son Aaron became rebellious during late teenage years. He rejected church, resisted correction, and eventually moved away emotionally from the family. Years passed with little visible change.

Ruth continued praying quietly.

Some nights she prayed through tears until exhaustion overtook her.

At times she wondered if her prayers even mattered anymore.

One evening, nearly twelve years later, Aaron unexpectedly visited home. During dinner he became emotional and finally confessed: *"Mom, I could never fully escape your prayers. Even during my worst seasons, I kept hearing your voice reminding me that God still loved me."*

Ruth realized something powerful that night:

Seeds survive drought seasons. And what looks dead externally may still carry life internally.

This is why mothers must continue praying even when circumstances appear hopeless.

Prayer is never wasted. Never.

Some mothers will see dramatic breakthroughs quickly. Others will witness gradual restoration.

Some may not fully see the harvest during their earthly lifetime. But Scripture repeatedly reminds us that God's work continues beyond human timelines.

Hebrews 11 speaks of people who died in faith while still believing God's promises.

Why? Because true faith understands something deeper than immediate results.

God's purposes extend beyond visible moments.

A praying mother's influence often outlives her earthly life completely.

Grandchildren may walk in blessings produced by prayers prayed decades earlier.

Future marriages may survive because of seeds planted by praying mothers.

Future ministries may emerge because someone refused to stop interceding.

Future generations may avoid destruction because one woman stood faithfully before God.

This is holy legacy. And perhaps one of the deepest revelations in this entire book is this:

The true power of a mother's prayer is not merely in changing circumstances. It is in partnering with God to shape destinies. That is sacred work.

The world may never fully understand its value. But Heaven does.

One mother praying faithfully may alter entire generations.

One atmosphere filled with peace may heal inherited trauma.

One woman choosing forgiveness may break decades of bitterness within a family line.

One surrendered life may become the turning point for generations yet unborn.

Never underestimate hidden obedience.

Never underestimate small faithful prayers.

Never underestimate tears surrendered before God.

Because Heaven sees differently.

And heaven records sacrifice carefully.

Malachi 3:16 says: *"A book of remembrance was written before him…"*

Imagine that. God remembers. People forget. Society moves quickly. Children sometimes overlook sacrifices temporarily. But God remembers everything offered through love and faith.

Every school lunch prepared prayerfully.

Every exhausted midnight prayer.
Every whispered blessing.
Every act of forgiveness.
Every painful sacrifice.
Every moment a mother chose faith instead of quitting.
Nothing is forgotten in Heaven.
And one day many mothers will fully discover how far their prayers truly traveled.
Perhaps this is why Galatians 6:9 remains so important:
"Let us not be weary in well doing…"
Why? Because weariness tempts people to stop sowing before harvest.
The enemy attacks weary mothers fiercely because exhausted people often lose perspective.
But this chapter is Heaven's reminder:
Do not quit praying.
Do not quit believing.
Do not quit sowing.
Do not quit blessing.
Do not quit standing.
Because what you planted in prayer will rise in power.
There are prayers still moving through Heaven's timing.
There are seeds still developing underground.
There are prodigals still being pursued by grace.
There are generational chains still breaking.
There are futures still being rewritten.
And there are testimonies still being formed from present tears.
One day many mothers will look back and realize:
The prayers they thought were weakest were actually strongest.

The tears they thought were unnoticed were carefully held by God.
The seasons they thought were barren were secretly building roots.
And the children they feared were lost were still being followed by mercy.
So to every praying mother reading this book:
Your tears will become testimonies.
Your midnight prayers are not wasted.
Heaven has heard every whisper. God remembers every sacrifice.
And what you planted in prayer will rise in power. Because a mother's prayer never falls to the ground.

Reflection Questions
What prayers have I become discouraged about?
Where have I mistaken silence for God's absence?
What seeds have I faithfully planted into my children and family?
How has God already sustained me through difficult seasons?
What legacy of prayer do I want to leave behind?

Practical Action Plan
Step 1: Continue Praying Consistently
Do not allow discouragement to silence your intercession. Keep bringing your children and family before God faithfully.
Step 2: Record Testimonies
Keep a journal of answered prayers, breakthroughs, Scriptures, and moments where God sustained your family.
Step 3: Speak Hope Over Your Home
Replace hopeless words with faith-filled declarations rooted in God's promises.

Family Exercise
Gather together and share one way each family member has seen God's faithfulness within the family journey. End by praying blessings over future generations.

Final Declaration
I declare that my prayers are not wasted.
My tears are seeds before God.
My home will become fertile ground for faith, healing, peace, and generational blessing.
Fear will not define my family.
Brokenness will not have final authority.
The God who heard Hannah hears me.
The God who protected Moses can protect my children.
The God who restored Peter can restore my family.
I will not quit praying.
I will not surrender to hopelessness.
I will trust God even in process.
What Heaven has promised will come to pass in God's appointed time.
My children belong to the Lord.
My generations belong to the Lord.
And what I have planted in prayer will rise in power.

Final Prayer
Heavenly Father,
Thank You for every lesson, every tear, every battle, every process, and every moment of grace throughout this journey. Thank You for reminding me that no surrendered prayer is ever wasted.
Today I place my children, my family, my fears, my hopes, my regrets, and my future into Your hands

again. Heal every wounded place within our home. Restore what has been broken. Strengthen what has become weak. Revive what feels weary.

Teach me to keep praying when answers delay. Teach me to trust You during hidden seasons. Teach me to believe that You are still working even when I cannot yet see visible change.

Lord, let my home become a place of peace, truth, healing, worship, wisdom, and godly legacy. Let future generations walk in righteousness because someone chose to pray faithfully today.

Protect my children spiritually, emotionally, mentally, physically, and morally. Draw prodigals home. Heal wounded hearts. Restore relationships. Break every generational chain operating against our family line.

And when my earthly journey is complete, may my prayers continue bearing fruit for generations to come.

In Jesus' name, Amen.

50 Prophetic Truths Every Praying Mother Must Remember

Revelatory Declarations That Shape Homes, Heal Hearts, and Build Generations

How to Use These Revelatory Truths

Throughout history, God has often used simple truths to release deep transformation. One sentence spoken at the right moment can strengthen a weary heart, restore broken faith, awaken spiritual vision, or shift the atmosphere of an entire home.

These 50 revelatory truths were written prayerfully to become more than inspirational quotes. They are spiritual reminders, prophetic reflections, and faith-building declarations designed to help mothers see their role through Heaven's perspective.

Many mothers spend years feeling unseen, exhausted, discouraged, or uncertain about whether their sacrifices truly matter. Yet Scripture repeatedly shows us that God works powerfully through praying mothers to shape generations, establish spiritual foundations, and redirect destinies.

As you read through these truths, do not rush.

Pause.

Reflect.

Pray over them.

Write them down.

Meditate on them.

Speak them aloud over your children and home.

Use them:

- ✓ at the beginning of each chapter,
- ✓ during personal devotion time,
- ✓ in prayer journals,
- ✓ as family discussion starters,

- ✓ for teaching or preaching,
- ✓ or as daily declarations over your household.

Some of these truths will comfort you.

Some will challenge you.

Some may heal wounds you have carried silently for years.

And some may become prophetic anchors you return to repeatedly during difficult seasons.

Remember this always:

A mother's influence is rarely measured correctly in the moment.

But generations often rise later because one woman chose to pray instead of quit.

1. *"A mother is a builder before she is a caretaker."*
2. *"Tears are liquid prayers."*
3. *"Children first grow in atmosphere before they grow in ability."*
4. *"The greatest inheritance is not property, but spiritual foundation."*
5. *"Prayer reaches where presence cannot."*
6. *"Some mothers carry nations in their womb."*
7. *"A mother does not just raise children; she releases destinies into the earth."*
8. *"What a mother builds in prayer, no circumstance can destroy in life."*
9. *"A child is first formed in a mother's prayer before he is formed in her arms."*
10. *"Behind every stable life is often a mother who refused to stop praying in unstable seasons."*
11. *"Invisible prayers create visible outcomes in children's futures."*
12. *"A praying mother is a silent force rewriting generational history."*

13. *"Before a child learns to speak, he has already been shaped by the words spoken over him."*
14. *"The home is not just a shelter—it is a spiritual atmosphere shaped daily by a mother's inner life."*
15. *"A mother's tears are never wasted; they are registered in Heaven as seeds of transformation."*
16. *"What enters a child's spirit in early years often speaks louder than what enters his mind later."*
17. *"A mother's prayers are not time-bound; they continue working even when she is no longer present."*
18. *"Every child is a prophecy waiting for a praying mother to give it voice."*
19. *"A home without prayer is not just quiet—it is spiritually unguarded."*
20. *"A mother does not only protect children from danger; she prepares them for destiny."*
21. *"Spiritual inheritance is stronger than genetic inheritance."*
22. *"What a mother sows in secret determines what her children harvest in public."*
23. *"Prayer is the only language that reaches a child in places a mother cannot physically go."*
24. *"A mother's voice becomes the internal echo her children carry into adulthood."*
25. *"God often answers a mother not by changing her circumstances immediately, but by shaping her legacy eternally."*
26. *"A praying mother may not see all her answers on earth, but she will see their fruit in generations.*

27. *"The spiritual climate of a home is often determined by the heart condition of a mother."*
28. *"A mother's hidden prayers become a child's unseen protection."*
29. *"Many children survive storms because someone was praying before the storm arrived."*
30. *"Children may forget gifts given to them, but they rarely forget the atmosphere they were raised in."*
31. *"The enemy attacks mothers fiercely because he fears the generations they carry."*
32. *"A mother's surrender to God becomes security for her children."*
33. *"When a mother prays, Heaven enters conversations she was never physically part of."*
34. *"Some breakthroughs arrive not because children prayed, but because mothers refused to stop."*
35. *"A praying mother sees beyond behavior and fights for destiny."*
36. *"Correction without prayer creates pressure; correction with prayer creates transformation."*
37. *"Children often drink emotionally from the well within their mother."*
38. *"A mother can shape a child's future long before the world recognizes the child's potential."*
39. *"What mothers normalize in the home often becomes what children pursue in life."*
40. *"Many destinies are healed when mothers choose forgiveness instead of bitterness."*

41. *"A mother's faith during hardship teaches children how to survive future storms."*
42. *"Before God changes a generation publicly, He often prepares a mother privately."*
43. *"The words spoken repeatedly in a home eventually become the beliefs children live by."*
44. *"Some mothers are carrying answers to prayers their ancestors once cried over."*
45. *"Prayer turns ordinary homes into spiritual training grounds for destiny."*
46. *"The enemy seeks to exhaust mothers because weary mothers stop building intentionally."*
47. *"A child's confidence is often built from thousands of small affirmations spoken by a mother."*
48. *"When mothers heal emotionally, generations gain freedom spiritually."*
49. *"The atmosphere around a dining table can shape a child as deeply as a classroom."*
50. *"Long after a mother's hands stop working on earth, her prayers continue working in eternity."*

About the Author
'GERARD ASSEY'

Gerard Assey is a Graduate in Economics, a PGD in Management (HRD) and holds a Doctorate in Leadership. Gerard holds several International Qualifications in Sales, Debt Collection, Training & Teaching, and is a 'Fellow' of the prestigious 'Institute of Sales & Marketing Management'-UK, a Certified NLP Practitioner, a 'Certified Trainer', an 'Accredited Management Teacher-Behavioral Sciences', a 'Certified Competency Facilitator', a 'Certified Management Consultant'- (the International credentials of a professional management consultant, awarded in accordance with global standards of the ICMCI); and a Certification from the University of Michigan in 'Successful Negotiation: Essential Strategies and Skills'

He is also a Member of the 'National Association of Sales Professionals' backed with several years experience in varied industries, both in India and Overseas. He also holds an 'Etiquette Consultant' Certification from the USA (by Sue Fox, Author of Best Seller: 'Business Etiquette for Dummies'. She has trained some of the top celebrities' world over). He was also a recipient of a scholarship for extensive training in Japan on 'Corporate Management for India'.

Gerard Assey is 'Founder & Chief Corporate Trainer' of the Group: '**Citius, Altius, Fortius Unlimited'**- an organization that **celebrated 20 years of Glorious Service** in 2021, focusing on 3 Core Competencies:

People. Performance. Profit; in functional areas of Sales & Marketing, HR & Organizational Development, covering Recruitment, Training & Consultancy!

Having managed organizations with large Sales Forces in India & Overseas, his specialization cover extensive areas of Sales Training (All levels - Presentation, Negotiation, Key/ Strategic Accounts Management & Managerial Skills for all sectors), Bid Proposal/ Capture Planning/ Management Trainings, Retail Sales, Customer Service & Customer Retention Programs, Training for Prevention & Collection of Debt, Self & Personal Development Programs (Time Management, Teamwork & Team Building, Business Etiquette & Personal Grooming, Leadership & Managerial Skills, People Management Skills, Train-the-Trainer etc), including preparation of Custom-designed Business Manuals for Internal (HR, Induction, and Sales etc) & External use (Instruction, User Manuals).

Gerard has successfully conducted over 6525 Trainings & Workshops (as of May '26) all across India, Middle East, Africa, Europe & S.E. Asia. Besides public programs conducted regularly, both in India & Overseas, he has some of the top names as clients whom he services from Single Owners to large Public & Government undertakings, covering all sectors, for their in-house needs.

His website: www.CollectionSkills.com is the only one in this part of the world to be featured in the 'Collections & Credit Risk Magazine-USA' under 'Who's Who in Training' and ranks TOP, along with other websites listed below on most search engines.

Gerard is author of 229 Books already (May 2026), all the books being available on all online platforms and outlets as E-books and Paperbacks

A few of our business related books:

1. Bite-sized Bits on Commonsense Management
2. Heart to Heart on Life's Principles'
3. How to become a Successful Manager
4. The Sales Professionals' Master Workbook of S.Y.S.T.E.M.S
5. The Professional Business Email Etiquette Handbook & Guide
6. The Professional Business Video-Conferencing Etiquette Handbook & Guide
7. Professional Presentation Skills
8. Exceptional Customer Service
9. Professional Tele-Marketing Skills
10. Professional Debt Collection Skills
11. The G.R.E.A.T. Sales & Service Workbook
12. Sales Training Advantage for Results (*The Ultimate Sales Training Manual to enable you stand out as a S.T.A.R.*)
13. CEO Daily Planner & Organizer
14. The Sales Professionals' Master Daily Planner
15. The Professional Debt Collector's Master Daily Planner
16. My Daily Planner & Organizer
17. MY EMERGENCY INFORMATION RECORD (Family Emergency & Peace of Mind Planner)
18. The Ultimate Therapist & Counselors Planner and Organizer
19. Building an Ethical Workplace
20. Managing Relationships at Work
21. Managing Business Meetings Effectively
22. Effective Delegation Skills
23. Goal Setting for Success
24. B2B Selling by Email
25. Professional Business Etiquette & Grooming
26. Dining Etiquette & Table Manners
27. Effective Networking Skills
28. Grooming, Etiquette & Manners for Teens, Young Adults & Future Leaders
29. Inter-Personal Skills
30. Get Ready, Get Hired!
31. Selling in a Recession
32. Effective Receivables Management in an Economic Downturn!
33. Real Estate & Property Sales Training
34. Credit Sales & Accounts Receivable Management

35. Selling Skills for Real Estate & Property Advisors
36. Take G.R.E.A.T. C.A.R.E!
37. Spa, Salon & Health Club Selling Skills
38. Selling Travel, Holiday & MICE Services
39. Selling Skills for Spa's, Salons & Health Clubs
40. Retailing in Salons & Spas
41. Selling Holiday, Vacation, Tours & Packages
42. The Power of Sales Referrals
43. Selling Luxury
44. Technical Selling Skills
45. Financial Advisors Sales Training
46. Dealing with Burnout at Work Monopolize Your Markets
47. Selling to Affluent Customers
48. Growing up with Grace
49. Financial Selling Skills
50. *The Effective Manager's Guide: Key Skills to Thrive*
51. From Aspiring to Inspiring: A Guide for New Managers on the Rise
52. The Power of Focus
53. Selling with Integrity: Sell Like Jesus The Perfect Role Model!
54. 31 Habits of Champions: Your 31-Day Journey to Greatness
55. Rejecting Grasshopper Talk: From Grasshopper to Giant-Killer-*Defeating Giants Daily!*
56. Navigate the AI-Powered Future of Bid & Proposals: Up-Skill to Stay Relevant with Alternative Career Paths & Opportunities
57. Hiring Sales Winners
58. Present with Impact
59. Success Unlocked: *Breaking Free from Habits that Hold You Back*
60. Complaints to Cheers, Feedback to Gold: Mastering Complaints Management
61. Thriving Together: *Cultivating Diversity, Equity, and Inclusion*
62. Coaching Skills for Sales Managers
63. Soaring to Success in Business & Leadership: Swifter, Higher, Stronger!
64. From Classroom to Podium: A Student's Guide to Powerful Public Speaking & Presentation Skills
65. Developing Self-Discipline
66. The CEO's 31-Day Power Plan: Unlocking Success through Essential Traits

67. Credibility Matters
68. A Winning Attitude
69. Bid & Proposal Management Using AI
70. Sales Forecasting: A Practical & Proven Guide to Strategic Sales Forecasting
71. Elevate & Energize: *50 Dynamic & Fun Activities for Peak Workplace Morale*
72. 'Sales SOS! Sales on Fire! *30 Days to Conquer Chaos & the Nightmares of Success!'*
73. Mastering Sales Managerial Skills: *Building High-Performing Teams & Driving Exceptional Results*
74. Eagle-Eyed Leadership: Unleashing the Power of 31 Lessons from Eagles
75. The Ultimate Employee Training Guide: *Training Today, Leading Tomorrow*
76. Being More Accountable at Work
77. Creating a Culture of Continuous Improvement
78. Effective Questioning & Listening Skills
79. The Power of Value Selling
80. The Growth Mindset
81. Mastering Professional Help Desk Skills
82. The Power to Lead with Empathy
83. Being Prepared: The Key to Unlocking Success
84. Youthful Spark-Youth Energizers, Activities and Games-Igniting the Fun in Youth
85. Ignite your Motivation for Success
86. Elevate Your Executive Presence: *Your Roadmap to Executive Excellence*
87. Smart Decisions: *Mastering Problem Solving with Strategic Solutions for Business Success*
88. Strategic Planning: *Developing and Implementing Strategic Plans to Achieve Long-Term Business Goals*
89. The Power of Stay Interviews
90. Developing G.R.I.T.
91. Adaptability
92. Diagnosis- *A Key Skill for Leadership*
93. The Burnout-Proof Salesperson: *The Master Guide to Preventing Stress & Burnout-* Strategies for Thriving in Sales
94. Learning from Failure: *Keys to Success*
95. Customer Success Management
96. Overcoming the Killers of Motivation
97. The C-Suite Code: *Mastering Skills for Executive Excellence'*

98. Dealing with Difficult Customers
99. Unlocking Your Potential: Mastering the Top 20 Life Skills for a Brighter Future
100. Nurturing Tomorrow's Leaders: *Essential Soft Skills Every Child Must Learn*
101. Lively & Fun Party Games for Seniors & Elders
102. Role Playing for Sales Champions: From Practice to Performance
103. Fun and Exciting Party Games for Kids
104. Case Studies for Sales
105. Role-Playing for Unbeatable Customer Service
106. Case Studies in Customer Service
107. Case Studies in Winning Negotiations
108. Case Studies in Management & Leadership
109. Case Studies in Human Resources & Talent Management
110. CEO Success Blueprint: The Essential Toolkit for CEOs and C-Level Executives
111. The Salesperson's Self-Coaching Guide: *Master Your Own Self-Coaching Plan for Success*
112. Overcoming Procrastination: *Your Ultimate Guide to Stop Delaying and Start Living Your Best Life*
113. When True Colors Are Exposed: *The Journey to Unmasking Humanity*
114. Life-Changing Habits for Teens: Teen Success Blueprint for a Bright Future
115. Workplace Stress-Free: *Proven Strategies to Thrive at Work and Beyond*
116. Objection Overruled: *The Ultimate Guide to Turning 'No' into 'Yes'*
117. Building Strong Teams: *A Comprehensive Guide to Team Building*
118. Ethical & Moral Leadership in Business: *Eliminating Unethical Practices & Building a Culture of Trust & Integrity*
119. Rising Strong: Building Positive: High Self-Esteem for a Fulfilling Life-*A Practical Guide for Students, Employees, Leaders & Entrepreneurs*
120 The Cheerful Mindset: Cultivating a Joyful Outlook Everyday
121. Leading Through Crisis: Case Studies on Crisis Management
122. Selling Beyond the Algorithms
123. MAGEN CAPD- Dialysis Record Journal

124. The Human Side of Healing: *A Master Manual on Professionalism, Patient Experience & Compassionate Care-From Treatment to Trust For Doctors, Nurses & Healthcare Teams*

From the Ministry side, Gerard graduated in the very first batch of Charis Bible College-India & had for over 9 years served as a Part-time Faculty at Charis Bible College-Chennai (Andrew Wommack Ministries-Colorado, USA).
He also holds a Diploma in Worship (a subject closest to his heart) from the JSOW and is also a graduate of the Advanced Mentorship Program (AMP) and the Circle Of Ministerial Engagement (C.O.M.E.) of Prophet Jerome Fernando and a Spiritual Son of the Esteemed Prophet.
An accomplished author of several Secular & Christian Books, Gerard has been on the board of a few international organizations and boasts of being the SON of the MOST HIGH GOD: An ordinary guy following an extraordinary GOD!

...And some of his most recent Christian Books being:

1. A Bouquet of Praises for My KING
2. Christian Jokes for the Serious Religious' Folks!
3. Jesus Healed You!
4. Praise24Ever! (also in Tamil version)
5. The 5G Network of GOD
6. Building Faith over F.E.A.R- FACE EVERYTHING AND RISE with JESUS
7. Hebrew and Greek Praise and Worship Words
8. Godly Mothers' and Grandmothers' Bible Story time for Kids!
9. Miracles of Jesus in Pictures
10. Raise your Praise all 365 Days
11. Thanking GOD with an Attitude of Gratitude
12. Meditating on the Attributes of GOD
13. Puppet Scripts
14. Alcohol Ruins, JESUS Reforms, Renews & Restores!
15. Habakkuk 2:2 Christian Daily Journal, Planner & Organizer
16. ABC of GOD's Word for Handwriting Practice
17. Daily Bible Verse Handwriting Practice (Building Godly Character & Faith through Cursive Handwriting Practice!)
18. Guiding Light: Fun & Faith-Building Bible Activities for Children
19. Rejecting Grasshopper Talk: From Grasshopper to Giant-Killer-*Defeating Giants Daily!*

20. Teen Titans of Faith: *Building Courage, Determination & Christ-like-Esteem*
21. I AM Empowered: *Unleashing Divine Power with Positive Declarations*
22. Be A Solution Provider-*From Passion to Purpose*: *A Biblical Guide to Being the Answer to the World!*
23. Miracles of JESUS
24. Parables of Jesus for a Meaningful Life!
25. A Grateful Heart: Importance of Sharing Testimonies of GOD's Grace
26. Melodies of Worship to JESUS: 31 Songs of Praise & Worship From My Heart to HIS!
27. I AM SO BLESSED!
28. My Daily Cup of Energizer
29. 31 Leadership Lessons *from* Jesus- *The Supreme Leader*
30. Peace Amidst Storms: A Biblical Guide to Conquering S.T.R.E.S.S.
31. Rise Above: 20 Biblical Eagle Lessons for Life's Triumphs
32. Godly Goal Setting: *The FAITHFUL Blueprint for a Purpose-Driven Life*
33. The Profound Attributes of our Mighty GOD: Understanding the 10S's of the Almighty
34. Worship Now, Worship Forever: *A Journey from Earthly Praise to Eternal Glory*
35. Unceasing Praise & Worship: *365 Days to Worship the King*
36. The ROAR Within: *Living with Purpose and Authority through the Power of the Holy Spirit*
37. From Potential to Purpose: Unlocking and Multiplying Your Talents & Gifts for Kingdom Impact
38. Songs from the Heart: *Worshipping GOD in Your Own Tune & Melody*
39. Awakening Praise & Worship: Hebrew & Greek Words to Raise Your Praise
40. Sing a NEW Song to the LORD Everyday: *Daily Devotions of Praise & Worship to Lift Your Heart & Glorify HIS Name*
41. *The* A.R.O.M.A. of True Worship: *Creating Worship That Delights God*
42. Becoming A Kingdom Champion: *Embracing God's Call for a Life of Purpose & Victory*
43. The Busy Businessman's Daily Devotional: 366 Crisp Truths to Start Your Day Strong
44. The Teacher's Heart: *Daily Devotions for Educators*
45. Anchored! *A 31-Day Devotional for Students Facing Life's*

Challenges

46. Suddenly! Unlocking Unorthodox Breakthroughs through Unusual Worship
47. Overcoming Adversity: *Lessons from the Bible for Modern Challenges*
48. LORD, Don't do it without me
49. Kingdom Leadership: *Biblical Principles for Modern Leaders*
50. Heartprints of God- *Growing God's Way:* Daily Devotions for Kids to Shine Bright
51. Send Judah First: Let your Praises Go up First to See the Mighty Move of GOD
52. DIVINE MOMENTS: *Recognizing, Embracing, Preparing, and Walking into Life-Changing Encounters with God*
53. Be a Builder in the Kingdom: *The C.E.M.E.N.T. Guide to Creating a Lasting Legacy*
54. Unshakable: *Pillars of Godly Womanhood* (Pillars of Faith That Changed History)
55. Lead Like a Shepherd: *14 Essential Traits for Pastoral Excellence*
56. The Worship Leader's Arsenal: *Powerful Exhortations to Ignite Thanksgiving, Praise & Worship*
57. Women of UnShakable Faith: *31-Day Devotional for Strength, Purpose & Influence*
58. Called to Teach: *A Complete 10-Week Training Guide for Impactful VBS Teachers*
59. Strumming for the KING: Cowboy Songs of Faith & Fire
60. The Ultimate Youth Camp Playbook: *50 Bible-Centered Indoor Games to Engage, Equip, and Empower Teens*
61. Glad in HIS Presence: *David's Revelation of GOD's Love & Mercy*
62. The Spirit Behind the Sound: *52 Devotionals for Worship Teams*
63. THE COWBOY'S COMPASS: *Riding the Trail of Faith with Grit & Grace*
64. Worship as My Weapon: *Living Victoriously through the Power of Praise*
65. A Worshipper Always Wins*: Living a Life of Victorious Worship*
66. Worship That Leads to the Throne: *Practical Strategies for Worship Leaders to Inspire Their Team & Usher People into God's Presence*
67. Worship as Warfare: *Conquering through the Sound of*

Surrender

68. Watchmen on the Walls: *A 31-Day Devotional for Worship Teams*
69. KINGDOM BUSINESS: *52 Biblical Principles for GODLY Leadership & Wise Decisions*
70. From Evening to Morning: *Rediscovering GOD's Sacred Hours*
71. Waves of Glory: *Worship through Dance, Flags, Staff & Sound*
72. WORSHIP TEAM BUILDER: *Guiding Your Team from Formation to Fruitfulness*
73. The Worship Leader's Master Training Manual
74. Skits for the King: Children's Plays for Every Church Occasion
75. Unbreakable: Building Strong Marriages and Families God's Way *(From Vows to Victory)*
76. Songs for my King: *A 31-Day Journey of Praise*
77. Building Powerful Children: *Raising a Generation That Will Shape the Future for God*
78. Character Before Chords: *The Heart of the True Worshipper*
79. 365 Days Before His Throne: A Worshipper's Daily Declarations
80. Broken to Built: *How GOD Restores Lives, Heals Hearts & Uses Broken People for HIS Glory*
81. Fear Did Not Come from God: *Discerning the Source, Dismantling the Stronghold & Walking in Power, Love & a Sound Mind*
82. THE GOD OF BEGINNINGS: *Positioning Your Life for What God Is About to Start*
83. HEALED ALREADY: IT IS FINISHED! Receiving What the Cross Has Completed!
84. A.D.D.E.D. Y.E.A.R.S. When God Overrules the Clock, the Diagnosis, and the Final Word
85. HALLELUJAH -The Sound That Heaven Understands *(Building a Life of Pure Praise)*
86. Worship in the Marketplace, Worship Beyond the Walls: *(Turning Work into Worship)*
87. ALPHA & OMEGA: *Living Secure Between the Beginning and the End*
88. JOYFUL NOISE: When Sound Becomes a Spiritual Statement (When Heaven Responds to the Sound of Faith)

89. F.A.V.O.R.: Five Dimensions of Divine Advantage
90. THE UNBROKEN LAMB: The B.O.N.E.S. of Divine Precision
91. YOU ARE A WEAPON: Unlocking the Power of Worship That Breaks Chains and Opens Heaven
92. M.A.G.N.I.F.Y. *Seeing God as He Truly Is—and Living Above Everything Else*
93. THE HEALING COVENANT: *God's Provision for Healing, Health, and Restoration of the Whole Body*
94. THE DEEP: *Unlocking the Hidden Supply of God Within You*
95. A Mother's Prayer: *The Hidden Power That Shapes Generations*

Besides regularly contributing to business & trade journals, including international ones such as the 'Creative Training Techniques' and the 'Sales News' of the U.S.A, He is also a member of several prestigious bodies & trade associations, having participated in many Conferences & Workshops in India & Overseas.

Prior to his last assignment of leading & managing a large MNC as head, Gerard had a 3-year stint in the Middle East as a Consultant with a leading British Consultancy Firm.

As the past 'Official Country Representative' for the International Business Award- 'THE STEVIES'-(the business world's own Oscar) for about 4 years- he ensured a few Indian companies that qualify for the same every year!

Gerard can be contacted at:

Email: training@Sales-Training.in,training@CollectionSkills.com
Websites:

www.Sales-Training.in
www.EtiquetteWorks.in
www.CollectionSkills.com
www.RetailSalesTraining.in
www.SalesTrainingIndia.com
www.ManualPreparation.com
www.TrainingWithPuppets.com
www.FirstContactAcademy.com
www.SalesAndMarketingRecruiter.com

www.ingramcontent.com/pod-product-compliance
Ingram Content Group UK Ltd.
Pitfield, Milton Keynes, MK11 3LW, UK
UKHW020050200726
13845UKWH00055B/627